Mission Entrepreneur

Applying Lessons from Military Life to Create Success in Business Start-ups

D0980654

By Jen Griswold

Praise for Mission Entrepreneur

This book is a MUST read for women everywhere who have big dreams and a heart to put family first. Jen Griswold brilliantly shares the significant challenges military spouses face, while providing actionable strategies on how to become their very own entrepreneur... the milprenuer. Women everywhere will love this book as Griswold inspires each of us to live, give, serve and grow, while becoming greater advocates for our beloved military community.

- **Jamie Petersen**, Co-founder, Team GiVe

As a military spouse and entrepreneur, this is the book I wish had years ago! Jen has such a giving spirit, and now she's giving her readers an incredible opportunity to soak up her wealth of knowledge!

- **Courtney Slazinik,** CEO, Click It Up A Notch (and a military spouse)

Jen Griswold reminds us that we already have the tools, and offers insights into a variety of paths to success, harnessing these tools and giving them new meaning and life. A must read for any "seeker" looking to expand beyond the mundane.

- **Jennifer LB Robins** of Predominantly Paleo, 4x bestselling cookbook author and Founder of Legit Bread Company (and military spouse)

So often I hear people say that they have a great business idea, but no idea what to do with it, or where to start. THIS is where to start. Through vast personal experience, insight from industry leaders, and advice from fellow entrepreneurs, you'll be moving from concept to profitable business in no time!

- Bridget Platt, CEO, Daddy's Deployed (and a military spouse)

Mission Entrepreneur is about following your dreams and reminding us that they sky really is the limit. Jen's story is the voice for all of the military spouses who refused to quit even though the odds were against them.

- Maureen Dougherty, CEO, Northeast Girl

Entrepreneurship is about creating solutions to big problems. As both a veteran and military spouse, Jen understands the difficulty faced by the family of military members. But she also understands the potential they have to create value for each other and for others while supporting their spouses. Jen provides practical advice to military spouses who want to have it all: build and own a business while still being a world-class partner to their military member/spouse.

- Eli Bremer, Air Force Officer & Olympic Athlete

Military spouses no longer have to feel trapped and isolated. Thanks to Jen Griswold they can dream bigger. She is there to help them forge a new path.

- Nicole Feliciano, Author of Mom Boss and CEO, Momtrends

Cover Design: Georgiana Goodwin
Layout & Design: Roberto Nunez

For permission requests, please contact the publisher at:
Mango Publishing Group
2850 Douglas Road, 3rd Floor
Coral Gables, FL 33134 USA
info@mango.bz

For special orders, quantity sales, course adoptions and corporate sales, please email the publisher at sales@mango.bz. For trade and wholesale sales, please contact Ingram Publisher Services at customer.service@ingramcontent.com or +1.800.509.4887.

Mission Entrepreneur: Applying Lessons from Military Life to Create Success in Business Startups

Library of Congress Cataloging-in-Publication has been applied for.
ISBN: (paperback) 978-1-63353-645-6, (ebook) 978-1-63353-646-3
BISAC category code:
BUS025000 BUSINESS & ECONOMICS / Entrepreneurship
FAM055000 FAMILY & RELATIONSHIPS / Military Families

Printed in the United States of America

There is no greater thing you can do with your life and your work than follow your passions in a way that serves the world and you.

- Sir Richard Branson

Dedication

To my Mom, thanks for instilling a spirit of service and an unwavering belief that I could make a difference in this world. Whether you realize it or not, your example is the inspiration for almost everything I've done in life. I love you!

To Jamie and Team GiVe and so many other sideline partners, thank you for making this story worth telling. Your dedication to yourselves and to your businesses proved my ideas could work. I couldn't be more proud to work with such amazing individuals!

To Kev, Cole and Ally, this book is as much yours as it is mine for all the extra help and support you gave me while dreaming it and writing it. I love you for believing in me!

In memory of our sweet dog, Tucker, who was my trusty sidekick for 14 years of this story.

Last, but certainly not least, this book is dedicated to all the military spouses who yearn to create and run something of your own. Your collective energy drove me to overcome my own fears and make this book a reality! Never give up on *you*, you're worth it!

Table of Contents

Introduction

I'll never forget the moment. It's etched in my memory forever. I was sitting on the floor with my two kids, ages three and one at the time. Both were in diapers, and both were sick. My husband had been deployed or on work-related trips off and on for the better part of three years during this particular assignment in California. I was exhausted. Mentally and physically. And if I'm being honest, I was extremely disappointed in where I had landed in life. I loved my kids and enjoyed being a reliable parent, but my personal achievement muscles were beginning to atrophy. The last three years had rocked my world and I had lost myself. And a terrifying thought kept running through my head:

"Is *this* all I'm destined for?" I used to have such big goals and dreams for myself. "Is this all there is for me now?"

It was from that very question and at that very moment that I resolved to make a change. For my family. For myself. For my future. The path ahead wasn't entirely clear at the time, but it was that specific moment of clarity on the floor that would lead me to the best discovery I would make: that I didn't *have* to be at the mercy of my crazy military life.

I had the power to create my *own* future. And it could happen through taking matters in my own hands and starting a business.

Silent Untapped Resource

As a distinguished graduate of the US Air Force Academy, a veteran, and an Air Force Reservist, I still shudder to think of how incredibly close I came to losing my identity and consequently my drive during the span of those three years. It was honestly one of the hardest times in my life, because I felt so out of place, unfulfilled, and generally unhappy.

Yet, my story is not unique to me. It is only one of thousands within the military spouse community that are similar in nature and belong to devoted spouses who silently grin and bear their hidden desires to find meaningful work.

In twenty years in the military, I have seen countless friends and colleagues make a valiant effort to keep a career going through their first few military relocations; however, after multiple attempts, qualifications that don't transfer from state to state, and the addition of kids, many just give up. Sadly, they decide their efforts are futile. This is especially true for families who endure relocations as often as every year, depending on the specifics of their military member's career field. With that kind of frequency, even if a spouse *does* land a great job, it is a major letdown to move to the next assignment and not find an equivalent position (or anything at all). After several rounds of this repeated scenario, confidence wanes and it's easy to begin to question one's self-worth.

As a business owner and problem solver, this employment dilemma perplexed me and left me wondering how to fix it. What's hard is that there is no denying that the military community is full of talent. Having interacted with hundreds of military spouses, service members and families in my personal life over the years, it's amazing to discover the hidden talents my military spouse sidekicks have picked up through their experiences. Here are just a few talents that could go on a resume for a large majority of them:

Quickly and smoothly relocates the family and kids to a new community at the drop of a hat...sometimes up to twenty times over the course of a career.

Endures long stretches of single parenting during deployments and job-related absences.

Organizes and leads large groups of other military spouses and family members with no formal training (and no pay).

Volunteers on base or post when needed.

Possesses ability to diagnose and complete household repairs (everything from fixing toilets to installing wood floors).

Yet even with all these amazing skills, jobs are still scarce.

Once I made the decision to pull myself out of the haze of my own unhappy situation, I started noticing just how few women in my military network were employed. At the time, most of us were in our early thirties, some with kids and some without.

My friends said they wanted to work and some truly needed the income, but *nobody* had jobs. It was obvious that something was wrong.

As I educated myself, I learned that up to 90% of military spouses are under- or unemployed (underemployed means a person is working for less money than their education would normally earn them). *Ninety percent*! Having witnessed this unfortunate employment scenario firsthand, I kept thinking what a shame it was to waste such awesome talent.

My Journey

Thankfully, I didn't allow the drab employment landscape as a military spouse to stop me from finding a better way. When I made the decision to return to the workforce, I naively wanted a job that only required part-time hours so I could be around for the kids, but that could still pay handsomely. Yet as I began my search, I quickly realized how difficult this was to find.

With my background and lack of recent work, it was nearly impossible to find an employer that would entertain a flexible arrangement upon entry. I wasn't willing to put my kids in full-time daycare, endure the high cost, and bear many hours of lost opportunity with them. So I did what my hard-headed logic often tells me to do, and I resorted to taking matters into my own hands. I decided that come hell or high water, I'd create the "perfect job" by starting a business and make my magical-high-paying-part-time job come alive!

With two children under the age of three, a husband who was in a demanding job, and a California house losing value by the second from a recession, it was definitely not a picture-perfect scenario. But as much as my head knew the cards were stacked against me, my heart responded even stronger with the resolve to make it happen.

And I did.

Putting in one late night after another, learning through failures, pushing myself into uncomfortable places, and unapologetically applying everything I had learned through life in the military, I found a path to success. What's more, it was like the whole world opened up to me. I learned. I stretched. I pushed. I fought. I grew. And through all of the haze of hard work, consistency, and dedication, I uncovered *me* again.

This stronger, more confident, and more determined "me" started dreaming again!

A Community with Skill

The beautiful thing with any hardship-to-success story is that you start to discover all of the stories in society that are just like yours and you begin to form your tribe. When I first started out in business, I hoped to find a mentor who was just like me. Someone with a similar background, someone who had already achieved success on their own, and someone who could guide me to do the same.

I was looking for military entrepreneurs.

Milpreneur

/mil-pruh-nur/

def: a veteran, military spouse, or member of the
military community, striving to build a business

&

LIVE . GIVE . SERVE . GROW .

In fact, I affectionately referred to them as *"milpreneurs"*
(military + entrepreneur = *milpreneur*). But unfortunately,
with a military spouse force that was chronically
underemployed and contained very few business owners, there
weren't any *milpreneurs* running in my circles.

Therefore, my only choice was to put my head down and
forge the way myself. My first venture was a self-grown home
staging and decorating business. I made it a game to race the
clock every day I worked, to make more money than I paid in
babysitting. The company grew from a small idea in my head
into an award-winning, locally-recognized establishment in
Northern California, fueled mostly by my will not to fail.

After four years, we moved across the country, I sold that company and was fortunate to be offered a unique opportunity to join the sales end of a rising skincare company during its infancy. There was unlimited potential for growth within the company, but my success would hinge on my ability to develop, inspire, and lead a team of independent consultants whom I would have to search for and find. With no sales or consumer goods background, this seemed a little daunting, and it seemed *way* outside my comfort zone...but after a lot of thought it hit me why I *had* to do it!

I remembered back to my days as an active-duty military officer and to how many times I was impressed by a particular colleague or their family member because of their activity, dedication, and hard work. Each time I would say to myself, "If I could run a business surrounded with the talents of people like this, it would be *so* successful!" Then I would mentally make a note to keep track of that person over the years, in case I ever decided to act on that thought. As I pondered how I would succeed in a business I knew very little about, I realized the solution was to leverage the talent of the untapped resources of military spouses!

My military peers would be the perfect business partners, because they had the resilience of mind, the work ethic, and the belief in teamwork they had learned from their military experiences. And boy was I right! In just six years in business, despite many of us relocating, enduring deployments, and working around single parenthood, we put our team of eight thousand independent sales consultants (comprised of many military spouses) to the test and grew to the top .1% of the teams within our company. Our success story spread wide enough that we even earned a spot on the NBC's Today Show!

Meanwhile, we weren't the only ones realizing the power of *milpreneurism*.

Occasional success stories began popping up in military circles all over the map. A successful fashion blogger living on a base in England, an upcycled military uniform handbag company started by two moms in North Carolina, a chronically ill spouse in DC who turned her survival story into a set of Paleo cookbooks...the stories began to emerge. They were incredibly inspiring and motivating, and they fanned my flame of determination more than ever to create a movement!

But what was even more fascinating was the fact that, from what I could tell, these *milpreneurs* were gaining success that was not based on any novel technique, new-fangled business model, or fancy strategy. Most of them didn't even have an MBA or business background. They were merely relying on what they knew best: the inherent skills and lessons they had learned through years of military life. These include skills like hard work, independent thought, resilient mindsets, the value of integrity, the importance of teamwork, leveraging the skills of those around them, and centering their work around a spirit of service.

I wanted to test my theory that the thread of commonality to their success was attributable to their military experience. So I dove into their stories and conducted interviews to find out what, specifically, about these secrets of military life was helping them pave their way to success. In doing so, my mind was opened to many more valuable lessons than I originally had imagined, especially surrounding *milpreneurs'* ability to live, give, serve, and grow while on their journey to success.

As I regained my identity along the bumpy and winding journey of becoming a *milpreneur,* the benefits of putting these secrets to work were life-changing. Now I get to coach women and help them create flexible businesses around their own busy lives. Over the past several years, I discovered that by giving back to women and helping them realize their potential as business owners, I could change the world a little bit every day. Even better, the women I coached were inspired to do the same.

So, I'm on a mission...a mission to give back to our country's amazingly talented military community by showing them the value of starting and owning their own business. Within these pages, I'll share with you some tips and inspiration to help you decide *why* to begin. I'll share some easy and low-cost options to get started. I'll provide insight into what worked for me and for other successful *milpreneurs* I interviewed. And in the end, I hope this book will spark you to pursue that old business dream that might have gotten buried after years of living through the daily grind. Dust it off, give it life, and go share it with the world. Who knows? Your one little idea could have a ripple effect that affects the world in ways you've never dreamt of. So let's get to it!

Here is a taste of what you'll learn in the upcoming chapters:

LIVE: So much of success lies in the journey. Find out how military spouses are finding ways to overcome their employment odds.

GIVE: We are always better together. When you center your business around the idea of giving rather than receiving, you tap into a deep well of inspiration.

SERVE: If you know WHY you're in business, you'll get there faster! *Milpreneurs* have a clear internal compass for service that drives them to do what they do.

GROW: Hard work works...with a strong work ethic and belief, success is always possible.

This book is meant to share *milpreneur* stories, to bring light to their underdog journeys, and to point out why we should encourage more *milpreneurism* to benefit the entire country. There is a lot to be learned from a life of military service. Within these stories there is strategy and application for any industry or business model. If *milpreneurs* can succeed with these simple secrets from military life, you can too!

Chapter 1

Waging War
on Underemployment

Entrepreneurial Roots

Business ownership runs in my blood.

I am the product of several generations of enterprising entrepreneurs, starting with my great-grandfather on my father's side. My grandfather was a World War II fighter pilot who, after completing his service, returned home to the state of North Dakota and began a legacy of business ownership.

It must have been an interesting predicament to come home from war and decide on a job. In fact, this is a tough decision that our exiting military men and women are still challenged with today. Let's face it: there are not a whole lot of traditional jobs that provide the same challenge and adrenaline rush that comes with flying a P-38 Lightning, dogfighting, and dive-bombing the enemy over the Pacific. But I imagine that my grandfather found business ownership and the autonomy that comes with starting something of his own to be a pretty close second.

Upon his return from war, my grandfather partnered with another WWII veteran and used his GI Bill benefits to obtain financing to buy John Deere dealerships in both Turtle Lake and Dickinson, North Dakota. After more than ten years in farm equipment sales, he went on to open his own insurance company with the help of my grandmother. For my grandparents, their insurance company provided a fulfilling career and also gave them an outlet to give back to their community (their company was a bedrock of their small community of farmers, oil field workers, and university personnel). In the end, their post-service start-up provided over forty-five years of support for their family and the local economy, while inspiring several generations of entrepreneurism in the future.

From my grandparents' success, three of their four children also went on to start successful businesses. My father was the oldest, and the first of the kids to venture into entrepreneurship. After struggling to find stability in his oil-related field of engineering, my Dad chose to start-up his own oil-related engineering business in the basement of our house in the small town of Laurel, Montana.

My bedroom was located adjacent to my parents' basement office, so I had a front-row seat to the day-to-day toils and tribulations of their start-up experience. I saw it all. I saw the hard parts of their start-up experience, like the long hours and constant responsibilities. But I also saw the incredible benefits, like the flexibility it provided my parents to be able to attend my sports competitions, no matter when or where they were. I was a witness to their hard work, and it gave me great respect for my family's legacy of entrepreneurship.

Unbeknownst to me, it would also teach me many lessons that would lend a hand in my success later in life.

The State of Military Spouses

Now, fast-forward thirty years. Once I transitioned from the active-duty Air Force to a more at-home role, I was able to engage in more activities with other military spouses. Suddenly, I was immersed in military life from a spouse's perspective. This was a turning point, where I realized *just how many* of the spouses around me were not working.

At first I just chalked it up to the fact that most of the women were raising kids and had chosen to stay home. Or maybe it was because we military families moved so much that people stopped trying to find jobs? Maybe it was just that military spouses didn't have the desire to work? But after three years of being home with my kids, trying to find the perfect job to fit around kids, military life, and moving, I realized that none of those statements were entirely true. It wasn't as black and white as I originally thought.

The work equation for military spouses is not a simple binary decision. There are a myriad of variables that go into whether a woman works or not. What I knew from chatting with my fellow spouses was that nearly *all* of my friends had the *desire* to work; however, the available options were not always a good fit. At that point, my eyes were opened to the fact that not only do military spouses need more creative and flexible options that work around their demanding lives, but they possess the very skills and perseverance necessary to create these opportunities themselves.

My hunch was confirmed once I began doing my research and looked into the numbers. And in fact, the numbers were more sobering than I expected. According to the Census Bureau's 2012 American Community Survey, 55% of spouses reported that they *need* to work and 90% reported that they *want* to work. Yet despite their desire and capability, the military spouse suffers from a 38% underemployment rate and three times the current civilian unemployment rate.[1]

The rate of military spouse employment is something the Department of Defense has monitored closely over the last twenty-five years, since it directly affects service member retention. Consistent research dating back as far as 1981 confirms that civilian military spouses of active-duty personnel work less and earn less money than non-military spouses of the same demographics.

The most recent research was completed in 2015 through the DMDC (Defense Manpower Data Center) Survey of Active-Duty Spouses and the Blue Star Families Annual Military Family Lifestyle Survey in 2016. Both provided some healthy insight. First, these surveys concluded that the large majority of spouses are females under the age of forty. This isn't shocking, but it does confirm that the large majority of military families are still quite traditional, with men in the role of the active-duty member and women as the spouse. Second, military spouses' educational achievements exceed the level of their civilian peers during important career-developing years. It is interesting to note that spouses gain four-year degrees at a rate of 5% higher than their civilian counterparts, from the ages of 25-30. In that same age range, military spouses also obtain graduate degrees at double the frequency of similar civilians. This is important, because it shows that the military spouse population is ambitious and capable of obtaining higher education at a pace that makes them highly desirable as employees.

Unfortunately, there is undeniable research demonstrating that despite their great qualifications, military spouses face higher unemployment than the rest of the country. The results will vary depending on which agency is measuring; however, all studies lead to the same conclusion. In 2010, a RAND Corporation study found that 12% of military spouses were unemployed.[2] Five years later, that gap rose. In 2015, the unemployment rate of military spouses hovered around 18%.[3]

That is more than three times the civilian unemployment rate for women over twenty!

And it gets worse.

Let's move away from unemployment, and consider the underemployment of military spouses. Based on the most robust evaluation of underemployment completed in a RAND study in 2011, a whopping 38% of military spouses were underemployed (compared to 6% of civilian spouses based on educational level).[4] This means that 38% of military spouses are employed in jobs not commensurate with their levels of experience or education. And to rub a little salt in the wound, they earn anywhere from 20-38% less than the average wage of their non-military peers in the same area of occupation.[5]

If it wasn't obvious before, this research highlights that there is a distinct problem. Military spouses want to work. Military spouses are capable and willing to work. However, military life creates numerous challenges to working in the traditional employment system. We know all this to be true. But questions remain: What can we do about this situation? And, why should the average American care about fixing this problem?

The Costs are Real

The reality is this bleak employment outlook for military spouses creates a culture of underemployment that costs the Department of Defense and the country dearly. A 2010 RAND study showed 42% of military spouses were not in the labor force.[6] Add the previously mentioned 38% underemployment rate to an 18% unemployment rate, and it creates a problem where a large majority of spouses aren't contributing to the country through earnings and income tax. That lost opportunity is actually a burden to the US economy and should create a sense of urgency regarding a need to remedy the problem.

When you break down the total lost income tax, unemployment benefits, and total health costs associated with unemployment, the unrealized bill it creates is absolutely astonishing. Experts estimate that the total estimated cost of military spouse underemployment is somewhere between $710,344,000 and $1,068,508,000.[7] A little alarming, right?!

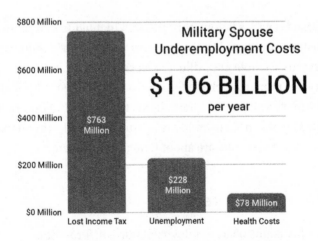

This may be a shocking price tag, but the costs don't stop there.

The other costs of military spouse underemployment may be less easily measured on a survey, but anyone in the military community knows they are real. One of them is the correlation between overall life satisfaction for military spouses (and family members) and service member retention rates. As a spouse, I can tell you for a fact that the statement, "a happy wife equals a happy life" rings true when it comes to longevity of service.

In the 2016 Military Family Lifestyle Survey by Blue Star Families, the top three concerns reported by spouses, active-duty members and veterans alike were "military pay/benefits," "change in retirement benefits," and "military spouse employment." The study went on to mention that the three most common reasons people left the military were military retirement (inevitable), completion of service obligation (also inevitable), and family reasons. Retirements and fulfilled commitments are inevitable and hard to control. But "family reasons" are very much within our control.

When spouses are satisfied with their work/life situation, they are much more likely to encourage and help their service member to continue their career in the military. In a blog post titled "Reflections in the Rearview Mirror," *milpreneur* and writer Angela Uebelacker describes being a military spouse and the challenges it brings to raising a family. She perfectly describes it as being "simply not that simple."

In fact, studies done on the civilian population show there is a direct correlation between employment and individual well-being. As the size of the overall military continues to dwindle and the operations tempo of deployments continues to remain intense, military spouse employment and its effect on retention will only increase in importance.

The other hidden cost is that of mental health. A life filled with military rigors inevitably gives way to things like depression, loneliness, addictions, and sometimes even suicide. Statistics tell us that twenty-two veterans commit suicide every day.[8] Unfortunately, the statistics for spouses and family members are not as closely tracked. But based on the frequency of other indicators, like calls to helplines and medical data, we know that mental health issues and suicides in family members have also increased as the operations tempo of the military has remained high through more than a decade of war.

Unfortunately, openness and honesty about suffering from mental illness is not highly looked upon within the military community. In fact, 41% of active-duty respondents in the 2016 Blue Star Families Survey said that they were uncomfortable seeking out mental health care from a provider in the military system. Additionally, 40% of survey participants felt that if they sought out mental health care programs or services, it could potentially harm their career.[9]

Finally, we have to recognize that under- and unemployment rates are not just gee-whiz facts for many military families.

They are a matter of survival. According to Blue Star Families, 47% of military families had two income-earning parents, which is significantly lower than the general US population, among whom 66% of households have two incomes.[10] As the cost of living rises, more and more military families need the extra income to survive. A 2014 article by ABC News indicated that over five thousand active-duty military families are eligible for food stamps.[11] Low-ranking enlisted families are the most at risk of falling prey to financial burdens without a reliable second income; however, even as the family of a mid-level officer, we had our own struggles in surviving on a single income.

After I left active duty, we were just barely able to cover the cost of our average California home mortgage. Given that at the time we bought our house in 2007, real estate prices had inflated to all-time highs, there was certainly no room in our budget for niceties like traveling, entertainment, or eating out. I remember I would panic at night thinking about any sort of catastrophe that would cost us more than a few hundred dollars, because we didn't have any extra cash to scrounge up should that situation arise.

To pass the time with as little spending as possible, I made it a game every day to take my two young kids on outings each day that cost no more than five dollars total. We had to get creative, but we eventually found our fun at the public library, the cheapest bakery in town, and in free public parks. I'm proud of the way we mustered through, but the extra stress and tension surrounding our finances during that timeframe is not something I'd ever wish on anyone, much less on someone whose sole focus should be on protecting our country.

The Answer Is Outside the Box

Thank goodness I'm hard-headed when it comes to getting something I want. In the case of my employment, I was determined to find the right kind of employment that would help me avoid the mental health traps I saw around me and to find something that worked around my family's needs, despite the fact that I had few examples of successfully employed spouses around me.

Once I realized that the answer was not in a traditional job, I became like a dog with a bone when it came to pursuing my business ideas. I didn't listen to the naysayers who second-guessed my decision. I put my head down, got determined, and found a way to make progress happen each and every day. If I hadn't been so hard-headed and determined, I may have ended up unemployed, unfulfilled, and bitter after years of frustrating attempts to find meaningful work.

When I began my hunt for the perfect, flexible job, I quickly realized that traditional jobs wanted traditional employees. The kind of employees that can be relied on for years. The kind who don't move away. And the kind that don't have lives filled with uncertainty like deployments, single parenthood, and extra stress. The traditional world of work sees our military "baggage" as something that makes us less desirable. After watching military spouses continue to unsuccessfully try to fit the mold of traditional jobs, I quickly came to the conclusion that our non-traditional lives will *never* fit the traditional mold. So why do we keep trying to fit our military square peg in the traditional round hole?

I began thinking. What if we took a step back and stopped feeling apologetic for the fact that we don't fit into the traditional work world, and embraced the lessons and blessings we've learned through our non-traditional lives? Perhaps the answer to the underemployment problem was not in the traditional work world at all. What if we took a clue from our grandparents, and took our employment destinies into our own hands? Not as employees, but rather as employers—entrepreneurs!

From Boots to Business

The concept of connecting business ownership to the military community is not a new one. In fact, my grandfather's story was just one of many from his era. According to the Institute for Veterans and Military Families at Syracuse University, after WWII, 49% of veterans started businesses with financial encouragement from the GI Bill. This carried through the Korean War where 40% of veterans continued the small business start-up tradition.[12]

Yet since 9/11, only 4% of the 3.6 million veterans who have served in the US have attempted a post-service small business start-up.[13] To put that in perspective, this 4% rate works out to 162,000 new veteran-owned businesses in 2016. In contrast, if veterans today were starting businesses at the same rate they did after WWII, that number would jump up to 1.4 million businesses. Additionally, since statistics show that veteran-owned companies employ an average of two additional veterans, we could logically estimate that in one year we could create another 2.8 million jobs for our country, simply from veteran business ownership.

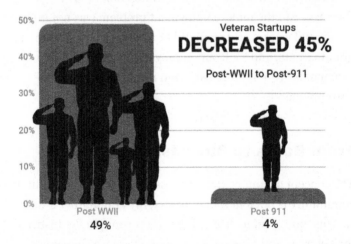

Veteran Startups
DECREASED 45%
Post-WWII to Post-911

Post WWII	Post 911
49%	**4%**

The reason veteran entrepreneurship isn't as widespread as during the post-WWII timeframe can be attributed to several possible factors. The first and most likely cause is that the post-9/11 GI Bill does not allow for low-interest loans like the version of the past provided. Another major factor is that after the economic crisis of 2007, it is much harder to obtain funding for small businesses. Since veteran-owned businesses are also

30% more likely to hire other vets, this lack of *milpreneur* start-ups has exacerbated the job creation problem over the last two decades.[14] This is evidenced by a 7% decrease in vet-founded businesses from 1996 to 2014.

The Start-Up Nation

But we shouldn't give up hope of seeing a new revival of military entrepreneurs. In fact, with the right mindset, we can create an environment that encourages the military community to capitalize on their strengths, to innovate, and to launch their own businesses. Imagine the positive ripple effect this could have right here at home!

Let's look to the country of Israel to see a great example of how military service and the hardships of military life have provided the perfect foundation for great entrepreneurs there. Israel is a country that relies on conscription (mandatory military service) to maintain a robust military. All Jewish citizens in Israel, both men and women, over the age of eighteen are required to serve in the Israel Defense Forces for at least two years. The normal length of service is a minimum of two years and eight months for men and two years for women.

Authors Dan Senor and Saul Singer studied the success of Israeli entrepreneurs in their book, "Start-up Nation," to uncover the secrets of how Israel, a war-ridden and relatively young country with a population of only 7.1 million people and no natural resources, could create more start-up companies than larger, more traditionally stable countries like Japan, China, India, Korea, Canada, and the United Kingdom. Their research discovered that when you combine the skills and resilience of military service, the persistence to succeed, a pay-it-forward attitude, and a spirit of "chutzpah," you end up with unparalleled economic development.

According to Google CEO Eric Schmidt, "after the US, Israel is the best" place in the world for entrepreneurs. Tech start-up Waze, a mobile satellite navigation application, and something I use daily to cart kids to and from after-school activities, was founded in 2007. It was the first Israeli consumer-app company to be bought for over $1 billion, and it helped to set the tone for building large tech companies in Israel. Waze allows millions of drivers to share real-time traffic and road info that can save others time and gas money on their daily commute. If you Google "Israeli start-ups in the US," you'll come across numerous lists of companies to watch in the coming years.

This is proof that with a strong history of military service, combined with a head-strong passion to succeed, you can literally come out of nowhere and create your own economic stimulus movement! Every military business owner is helping in this movement. And with a tribe of *milpreneurs*, social influencers, and supporters with a shared vision, we can foster the right environment to change the world right here at home. In fact, the military community has the skills, network, and manpower to make the US an even better Start-Up Nation!

Why the Most Portable Job is a Business

The reasons business ownership works well with military life are numerous. With a shift in commerce from big corporations to smaller, more nimble business models, there has never been a better time in history to be an entrepreneur. With more and more brick-and-mortar stores trading their physical spaces for more agile virtual business models, the opportunities for the everyday entrepreneur are endless.

Could you have ever imagined that one of the biggest retailers in the country would get the large majority of their revenue from online sales?

Kudos to Amazon.

Could you have ever imagined that one of the most successful taxi companies wouldn't own any cars?

Kudos to Uber.

Could you have ever imagined that one of the largest vacation rental companies wouldn't own any hotels?

Kudos to Airbnb.

And could you have ever imagined that one of the most popular methods of watching movies wouldn't include a theater or a DVD?

Kudos to Netflix.

These cutting-edge companies prove that business ownership is changing rapidly with the times. Hence, there is no time like the present to take advantage of this evolution and build a business that you can custom-design around your specific life needs.

Small business ownership provides unmatched flexibility and a variety of logistical options for how to set up your operations. For me, it provided the flexibility to work around the challenges of raising small children despite unpredictable deployments and frequent relocations. There was no other job out in the market that I could have obtained that would have allowed me the flexibility I needed to work around naps, babysitter availability, and my hubby's flying schedule. Over the course of ten years in business we have relocated to three different states, my kids have migrated from preschool schedules to full-time school schedules, and my husband has been promoted in rank three different times. Through it all, my business allowed me to flex along with each and every phase.

Along with incredible flexibility, being a business owner also allowed me to maintain my job as "Mom" as my #1 priority. As much as I was driven to grow my business, I was also very sensitive to making sure I was always there for the little moments with my kids. I will never forget the pictures etched in my memory of bringing my kids with me to work when I was decorating homes. Most of those memories involve them sitting strapped in their car seats with big smiles on their faces, with faux foliage and other essential home staging décor packed all around them. Once we would arrive at a job, I could give them harmless tasks like moving plants and folding blankets as their way of helping to complete the work.

Not only was it handy to bring them with me on jobs to avoid daycare costs, but it allowed them to see their mom pursuing goals outside of the common homemaking tasks. I have always cherished that from a young age; my kids were able to see me not only as their Mom, but also as a smart, capable, and driven woman that they could look up to and be proud of.

Another major advantage to business ownership today is the fact that technology is something anyone can leverage. Amazingly, technology has evened the business playing field and is providing access to business opportunities for more and more everyday entrepreneurs. With each new passing day, I also recognize how incredibly capable the next generation is with all these new technological advances.

The Millennial generation has been raised in an era where video, internet, and Wi-Fi are all they have ever known, making them more connected and more capable than ever before. When I graduated college at the turn of the millennium, cell phones were just becoming popular, but they were large and had antennas and there was nothing smart about them, since the internet itself was just gaining traction. I giggle at memories of "chatting" with my husband on a blue DOS screen where we made our own version of an emoji face with the shift key and punctuation <grin>. It is absolutely incredible to think of the giant strides in technology that have occurred in the last seventeen years.

Today, a young entrepreneur can literally use the power of a smart phone to run a variety of convenient small businesses. And most likely, any business they choose will leverage the power of social media to do work for them at all hours of the day or night. There is also a strong possibly that his or her business will occur in multiple countries across the globe and in multiple languages. In today's world, all this could happen from the palm of your hand, with you still in your PJs, sitting comfortably on the couch. The power of technology today is literally mind blowing. And it's providing much needed empowerment to the *milpreneurs* who deserve it!

Chapter 2

Ten "Secret Weapons" in Business

I have always been an entrepreneur at heart.

In fact, some of my earliest business memories as an elementary student are of putting together "junk stores" on my front steps. There, I would sell all the prizes that I had earned at the school store for good behavior and top grades. I would bring home my weekly collection of pencils, scented erasers, and stickers (back when those were a "thing"), and display them on the front porch with a homemade "open" sign. I had the advantage of being one of the oldest kids in the neighborhood, and thankfully my little sister and her friends looked up to me, so my junk store had immediate legitimacy.

Like any smart businesswoman, I tested my prices out on the local market. I played with how much the kids in the surrounding houses would pay to bring home my wares. One would think they wouldn't have much value, given that anyone could earn the prizes themselves for free. But what I found was astonishing! I hit the jackpot with my elementary school customers; they wanted to buy it all! Not only was it fun to have eager customers, but they also taught me my first lessons in presentation and viral word-of-mouth marketing. If I made sure my goods were arranged in an appealing and organized manner *and* I took good care of the "well-connected" kids on the block, they organically spread the word and business stayed steady.

Given my exciting success, I experimented with adding other random "junk" items to my list of offerings; like Halloween candy I didn't like and rocks. Yes...rocks! Straight from the back yard to my store. Apparently, that was the point where my greed had gotten the better of my business plan. Before I knew it, the mother of the children who lived next door leaned out her door with her finger up pointing at me, yelling, "My kids will not be buying anymore of your overpriced JUNK!"

That ended the junk selling, but it certainly did not stop my love for entrepreneurism. Whether I played piano for tips at Christmas, sold tickets to family to watch backyard plays I produced with my cousins, or sewed the simplest purses for sale, I was always dreaming up something! I don't remember my parents particularly encouraging my ideas, but they certainly didn't quash them either.

As I grew up and began life as an adult, my business ideas shifted to focus on what I could do to help the military world around me. First, there was my big idea to open a coffee hut called the "Daily Grind." Then, there was my idea to create a series of binders for military families who needed to keep track of different categories of documents. There was also my attempt at securing military base aerobics contracts. And I even toyed with how to create a work-from-home business that would sell fashionable workout clothes. By now, almost all of these ideas have been accomplished by someone else (you're welcome for the leggings idea, LuLaRoe!), but I like to think my ideas were ahead of my time.

While I was fortunate to start my entrepreneurial journey as a child, as I gained more experience in business I observed that many of my business-owning peers started later in life. Most often, their business ideas would form around their passions and how they could solve problems they saw within the world. I also noticed that many of my friends were propelled by the confidence they had gained through their military experiences.

And then it dawned on me.

Maybe it wasn't just my lifelong interest in business that helped me gain success. Perhaps the military life I had been a part of for the previous ten years also played a big hand in providing me with the right set of skills to be an entrepreneur?!

As I thought through this idea on a deeper level, I realized there were many reasons why military life was conducive to business ownership. In fact, they were really strong reasons, too...so much so that I eventually named them "secret weapons." Let's take a look at the top ten "secret weapons" from military life that creates great entrepreneurs.

Top Ten "Secret Weapons" (from Military Life) That Create Great Entrepreneurs:

1.   The Powerful Military Network

It is common to hear that business is all about "who you know." Fortunately, the military community is one giant network of great contacts. With each new move or Permanent Change of Station (PCS), a military family meets a whole new set of people through work, school, base neighborhoods, church, and other community organizations. People who retire from the military usually move at least a handful of times, creating a large network of similarly suited contacts.

Word spreads quickly within the military community once they recognize the value of a great product or service on the market. In fact, "word of mouth" marketing is actually an organic process in military networks. Why? Everyone heavily relies on the opinions and suggestions of their counterparts. In fact, every time we find out we are relocating to a new area, the first thing we do is think about who we already know there and ask them for their recommendations.

The first three questions I always ask are:

- "What are the best schools in the area?"

- "Do you have a favorite hair stylist and how much do they charge?"

- "What is your favorite restaurant?"

The fun part about all this is that military families love to share their favorites. So, when any entrepreneur develops his or her business concept, your local military network is an invaluable resource for marketing! Additionally, because military families are frequently on a regular relocation cycle, their connections extend far and wide across all continents, allowing for quick expansion. Having "boots on the ground" in simultaneous markets can allow for quick growth into multiple areas.

When I launched my social commerce business in 2010, I didn't exactly know whether it would work. But I *did* know that it had a lot of utility for military spouses. The business model was lean, it did not need a lot of inventory, and the marketing was done by leveraging the power of social media. That created a huge opportunity for portable work, if people could digest the concept and get over the stigma of similar business models of the past. That left the big question: would my network want to share the message?

Despite my concerns, I jumped in and gave it my all. In just six years, my organization blossomed from a party of one to an organization of over eight thousand entrepreneurs spanning six continents, fourteen time zones, countless military bases and producing over eighteen million dollars annually. Even though the number of civilians on the team now outnumbers the military members, the military values of hard work and being a part of something bigger than yourself have permeated everything we do. Our team has rallied around the idea that being able to serve others with business success is far more motivation than merely just earning a paycheck. I truly believe that the majority of our early growth would never have been possible without the power of our military mindset and the connections within my military network.

Knowing all this, don't be shy to put your network, whether it's military or not, to work. As you are developing your business concepts and ideas, use your Rolodex (that's a contact list, for you Millennials) to reach out and share the details of your business plan. You might be surprised at how eager they are to help you! Describe your ideal client in detail, so your well-connected colleagues and friends can be your eyes and ears in their community and help extend your business ideas quickly.

2. The Beloved US Military Brand

Brand names like Apple, Nike, Starbucks and Chick-fil-A all provide a sense of trust and reliability, no matter where you visit them. They are brands you can depend on without a second thought. The same is true of the United States military community.

As a member of this community, the rest of the population holds you in high regard as a person that is reliable, trustworthy, loyal, and disciplined. Investors, clients, supporters and even your competition give you instant credibility due to your years of military experience. It's not just "civilians" who hold military businesses and employees in high regard. According to the *Harvard Business Review*, military consumers are recognized for their affinity to buy from other military businesses. This support is "rooted in institutional culture and reinforced" by members of the community whether it's with purchasing power or hiring power.[15]

While other small business owners have to work tirelessly to build that type of trust, military entrepreneurs and businesses who hire military veterans get the privilege of having it organically right from the start. Military entrepreneurs have a unique opportunity to create businesses that seek to hire fellow military community members. As colleagues who can interpret the unique skills and abilities of a military spouse or service member's resume, you have the pick of the litter when it comes to hiring and building something that can truly leverage the power of the military brand. So, use it strategically to increase the speed of your growth.

3. One of the Best Investments

As a trustworthy, driven and reliable individual with the backing of the military brand, people are eager to help you succeed. Whether it is veteran resources, scholarships, higher education or loans, there are ample opportunities if you just look.

If you are looking for a modest amount of funding, I recommend you begin your search by looking at a range of nontraditional investment options for small businesses. Often, they are quicker, easier and less stringent to obtain than traditional bank financing for a small business. Some examples are crowdsourcing, microloans, and angel investors.

I remember lying in bed at night, thinking about my big dreams of starting my first business. I was ready to launch, but the timing for us financially couldn't have been worse. I had just transitioned from the active-duty Air Force to the Air Force Reserves, and I was only working one weekend a month. On top of that, were burdened with a hefty mortgage in California, right before the housing crash caused the value of our home to plummet. We were in a tight financial position, to say the least.

Even though I knew my idea to start a decorating business for military families was viable, the thought of scraping together a thousand dollars to get a certification in home staging was daunting. I looked at business loans, but there weren't a whole lot of options for less than ten thousand dollars and the thought of taking on more debt was even more depressing. Thankfully, I found a way to fund the training by selling a few household items online. But I will never forget that feeling of helplessness knowing I had an effective business idea that I was willing to work for, but had no funds to get started.

So when I began my second venture in 2010, I made it a priority to find ways to give back to the start-up businesswomen like me who just needed a little kick-start to get themselves on their way. I partnered with a young branch of a national lender, Accion, in San Antonio, Texas. I asked them to earmark my donations for military women who wanted to start small businesses. Then, those donations became small loans that, along with Accion's development program, helped businesses get off the ground.

After many months of donations, I received a letter from the first woman who had been able to launch her business with my help. It was, by far, one of the most rewarding moments of my life. The recipient was a military spouse and sent pictures of the opening day in the yogurt shop she opened with the help of her Naval husband. The smile on her face in the picture put an even bigger smile on mine. Plus, it provided more motivation to grow my own business, so I could give back even more in the future. And it reinforced the idea that our military community is worth the investment.

So as you begin your journey, don't be shy when you are seeking capital to get started. You might be surprised at how many individual angel investors within the military community may have an interest in your success as well. The bottom line is this: the money is out there...be diligent and creative, and you will find your funding source!

4. Broad Range of Experiences

Being an entrepreneur means that you are required to wear many hats: CEO, bookkeeper, fundraiser, sales manager, secretary, customer service specialist, and marketing expert, just to name a few. Unfortunately, a lot of times visionary business owners can lack the self-control, confidence, and breadth of skill to be able to succeed in a position with so many requirements.

It is no secret that military life puts families and members through a vast array of experiences. As a result, they are adaptable to change and are very confident with making tough decisions in unfamiliar environments. Experiencing a lifetime of change, involving a combination of military moves, combat deployments, single parenthood, and rebuilding lives in new locations, makes a person very independent and confident. That confidence and decisiveness are also the same skills necessary to be a successful entrepreneur.

I started my first business while juggling a newborn (days old) and a two-year-old. What possessed me to start at this particular moment, I will never understand! But I did. And I loved the challenge.

Thankfully, my resilient nature, after enduring so many years of moving, deployments, and chaos, helped me handle this season of craziness. My husband was often traveling during my business start-up period, so the schedule was pretty hectic. When he was gone on trips, I was a one-woman show. I would work a full day of decorating homes, feed the kids dinner, put them to bed, and *then* I would begin hours of administrative work for my business. Needless to say, I never saw any TV during those start-up years. But I truly believe that my experience and resilient state of mind were what led to my eventual success. And I attribute all of that to the many lessons military life taught me.

5. Awesome Work Ethic, Discipline, Problem-Solving, and Decision-Making

According to *Bloomberg Business*, eight out of ten business owners will fail by their eighteenth month in business.[16] The *New York Times* cites one of the top reasons for failure as "operational mediocrity."[20] Fortunately for those in the military community, years of structure, disciplined decision-making, and developing a stellar work ethic help increase a person's odds of success. Ask any corporate recruiter why they love to hire military spouses, veterans, and family members. Unequivocally, it's because they have a dedication to work that is unmatched!

Additionally, when you move as frequently as many military families do, you don't survive without the ability to make sound decisions and problem solve. For example, when traveling cross-country from California to our new assignment in Virginia, we were forced to be quick on our feet when we learned our rental house would not be available to move into until nearly a month after we arrived. It wasn't financially feasible to live in a hotel for that long, so we made some strategic phone calls and found a family friend who had an extra couple of bedrooms that were available. These strange twists and turns to normal life may be perceived as devastating or depressing to anyone else. For us, they equate to some of our favorite memories of family bonding through unexpected circumstances. And, added up, they built a foundation of great experience to prepare me for the constantly changing environment of business.

6. Capitalize on Your Benefits

While many entrepreneurs have to endure a scary start-up period where their investment capital may be utilized to the point that there is nothing left for medical benefits, such is not the case for military entrepreneurs or employees. With access to reliable healthcare, dental and life insurance benefits, military entrepreneurs can feel safe in knowing they won't have to forgo routine care or pay outrageous bills to get their business off the ground.

Add to that the awesome educational benefits provided by the Montgomery and Post-9/11 GI Bills, and a person can set themselves up with a foundation for business success without having to go into debt, like so many others. These benefits are not just for the military member or veteran, but can also be transferred to spouses and family members.

Additionally, there are other sources of income, such as Tuition Assistance. Or the MYCAA (Military Spouse Career Advancement Account), which is a $4,000 allotment provided to spouses in certain eligible ranks to obtain training towards a "portable career." Whether these programs provide a basic degree or more specialized training in an area of business, they are too valuable to leave unused if you have a business idea you'd like to pursue.

7. Certifications, Security Clearances, and Background Checks

If there is one thing that is for certain, it's that military folks are recognized as upstanding citizens. Between specialized work experiences, educational opportunities, volunteer requirements, and background investigations, most military members have been vetted numerous times by numerous different agencies during their military experience. Obtaining these investigations and clearances is a costly process, sometimes to the tune of thousands of dollars. Having access to this type of vetting gives military entrepreneurs a major advantage they wouldn't otherwise have. And it makes them highly desirable as candidates to work for or to start a business that requires higher-level clearances or background checks.

The simple benefit of having base access and higher-level security clearances can play a role in opening up jobs or contracts that others do not have. One of my first big decorating contracts was with the housing company that ran the base housing on Travis AFB in California. Because I had a military ID and could quickly and easily navigate to and from the base, it most certainly made my proposal for work seem more appealing. It also cut down on the time it would take any other company to complete the constant flow of decorating projects the job required.

My favorite project we did there was a home makeover for a deployed family. Many stores in the local area donated furniture and accessories to help us complete a whole new look for their home. Upon the reveal, there were tears of joy and surprise and they were so grateful for their new look. That special moment will forever remain as one of my favorite memories of being a business owner! And it made me extra grateful to have the background checks and clearance to be able to be considered for that project.

8. Organization and Planning

Just like with any important venture, when you're in the business of moving a lot, like most military families, you have to be organized and have a good process for planning. Whether it's moving to a new community, starting kids in a new school, or working through a deployment, it doesn't work very well if you don't have a well-thought out plan. Over the years, I've watched many friends and colleagues hone their system down to a science. Some even go to the extent of making checklists and binders to keep their process on track. Then, each new relocation allows for another chance to tweak and perfect the system.

But not all of us in a family are completely type-A personalities who find joy in making checklists. So, we also have to be good at recognizing each family member's strengths and weaknesses and prioritizing where they can be best utilized in the process.

What better practice for business ownership, right? In any type of business, there will be a variety of strengths and weaknesses within your team. A good leader has to recognize the strengths of each of the members of their group; the creative one, the detail-oriented one, the one who is good with people, or the one who has a knack for making things look good. When you can quickly recognize how to best utilize the strengths of each team member, the faster and more effectively you'll accomplish your goal.

9. Culture of Teamwork, Trust & Accountability

One of the most valuable tenets of a good military unit is the ability to operate with teamwork and trust. The importance of both can literally be a matter of life and death. Consequently, the ideas of collaboration and working together permeate every facet of military life.

It's second nature to repeat the same process when building a cohesive business team. Like a military team or unit, it's natural to bring a team together to rally around a business mission. And a good leader recognizes that each team member's specialized skill is equally important in getting the job done.

There are a lot of people who would describe corporate business environments as "cutthroat" and "all about the money." But it certainly doesn't have to be that way. And in my experiences with working with other military entrepreneurs, it isn't. In their organizations, it is still "all about the team," and people enjoy being a part of that mindset! Plus, when everyone is on the same page, it still achieves great things for the bottom line.

Now, we all know that things won't always go perfectly when growing a start-up. Luckily, anyone in the military community is used to holding something or someone accountable to errors. In battle, when something goes awry, an after-action report reveals what happened and who needs to take the proper course of action to fix their part of the problem. Any good business owner knows that mistakes are an important part of the journey and that the faster you can learn from your mistakes and hold yourself and your team accountable, the faster you will grow. Military folks already know how this works!

10. Solid Values, Sense of Purpose, and Loyalty

Finally, one of the biggest advantages of military life that can be applied to business is that we are driven with a sense of purpose and a set of deeply rooted values that serve a higher purpose and calling. Whether that means upholding principles of democracy, a desire to protect family, keeping military traditions, or building camaraderie (i.e., band of brothers), each of us has something that drives us beyond simply a paycheck. This way of thinking and loyalty to one another creates an environment of incredible commitment. But it's a commitment much deeper than most "jobs," because the motivation to do well runs far deeper than just numbers in a bank account.

In the business world, this kind of higher commitment can be likened to the concept of social entrepreneurism, which has gained immense popularity over the last decade. Yet, in the military it has always been a way of life.

The *Oxford Dictionary* defines a social entrepreneur as:

"A person who establishes an enterprise with the aim of solving social problems or effecting social change."

The military community is committed to achieving a greater good and enlisting themselves to the service of something bigger than themselves. That is a powerful platform if used correctly. For instance, giving free advice, supporting local causes, and making gratitude a part of business are common practices in the military community, but they are concepts that may seem novel to some business owners. Yet, anyone can implement this type of selfless mindset in any business. In fact, building a business that has a mission beyond just making money is one of the main reasons why good social businesses gain momentum and succeed.

So, embrace your labels as military spouse, veteran, reservist, or military member and go seize the day building a business around your passion. I can't wait to see how your military background, your passion, and your dedication to serve will manifest itself in your efforts as a *milpreneur*!

Chapter 3

WHY-Centered Business

A Good Business Begins With WHY

Multiple studies show that 70-80% of Americans hate their job![18] Does that surprise you? Many employees continue in jobs they dislike because it is «safe» and «routine.» For those brave entrepreneurs who are willing to take risks and start a business of their own, their respective work experience is much more fulfilling, since they are passionate about what they are accomplishing. Unfortunately, as a member of the military community, we have had years of training to minimize and eliminate risk. Many of us struggle to overcome the intimidating choices which surround starting a new company or business venture. After years of learning to recognize and reduce risk, it takes new tools to enable us to prevail over our risk adversity and to embrace the challenges entrepreneurship will undoubtedly bring.

The first and often scariest obstacle to starting a business is trying to figure out what exactly you want to do. There are so many decisions to ponder. What type of business will you choose? What type of business model? What product or service will you sell? How much will you charge? Is the business scalable, etc., etc.? The questions can go on and on. As a new entrepreneur, you can spend countless hours trying to find the perfect answers. But when you really boil it down, deciding what business to start is actually easier than you think.

It may sound a little bit Yoda-like, but the answers to your start-up questions aren't found in books, or via business consultants, or on websites. Rather, the best place to look for the answers is within you. The answers are deep within your sense of self and they form a vision that is driven by your passions. This undeniable force is called your WHY. It's your inner compass. It's your personal North Star. Your WHY is the gut feeling that tells you exactly what fits and what doesn't. It will guide you and lead you through many tough choices and decisions throughout your business. But unlike a lot of your business decisions that will be led by your data-driven brain, your WHY will be defined by your heart.

After having been successful in business for several years, this concept was reinforced for me when a friend of mine recommended Simon Sinek's book, "Start with Why: How Great Leaders Inspire Everyone to Take Action." This is now one of the books I recommend to every entrepreneur beginning their business journey. Sinek presents a simple yet powerful way to align your beliefs, strategies and your passions to build an inspired business. Unbeknownst to me, I had been executing a lot of what Sinek describes in his book without even knowing it.

I have always believed in following my heart while building my businesses. There were many times that I made decisions that "felt" right, but which I couldn't rationally explain to my husband or colleagues in a business plan. Yet, after reading Sinek's book, I realized that he was putting words to what I had always done. For instance, when I first started my design business, anyone could have argued that it didn't make sense as I didn't have any formal education or experience in the field. And you know what? I would have agreed with you if it was just decorating for anyone. But in my case, the business truly came about because I knew that military families move so often, that many times they don't get the time or help they need to properly decorate their ever-changing residences to get that "homey" feel. My business would fill that void. And my WHY was to help military families. Decorating homes would just be the vessel to get there.

Similarly, when I started a second business, which was essentially teaching and coaching entrepreneurs how to personally grow markets with a leading skincare brand, I started working with my company because I could see another path for helping military families by employing military spouses. I didn't know the first thing about skincare or sales before I started. But I saw a natural path for how the business could support my WHY. I was most certainly thinking with my heart, not my head, or I'm certain I would have found a lot of data to sway me otherwise. Thankfully, my WHY has guided me through my entire business journey.

Likewise, military members often talk about WHY we serve our country. When you ask a veteran or currently serving military member why they wear the uniform you're likely to hear a myriad of reasons, from protecting the Constitution, to serving alongside the men and women within their unit, to making the world a better place for their children, and so on. These deep and meaningful reasons are often very personal, and reflect why the members of the military and their families are willing to make the extraordinary sacrifices they do.

Those of us within the military community rely on our WHY to push through challenging times; similarly, none of my businesses would have succeeded if my purpose hadn't been so strong. Therefore, I think it's worth investing some time to understand your WHY when it comes to entrepreneurism.

Use the Golden Circle to Guide You

One of the powerful concepts that Sinek presents in his famous TED Talk, "Start With Why," is called the Golden Circle. The Golden Circle is based on an age-old principle called the Golden Ratio. In the world of the arts, (like architecture, design, and painting), the Golden Ratio is thought to provide an equation to determine a perfectly symmetrical relationship between proportions. The Golden Ratio is given credit for beautiful designs throughout history. In fact, some people argue that the Golden Ratio is what builders used to create the Great Pyramids, as well as famous ancient Greek architecture.

Sinek, however, uses the concept of the Golden Ratio to create what he called the Golden Circle. In the Golden Circle, there are three concentric circles that correspond to the three primary levels of the brain.

The Golden Circle

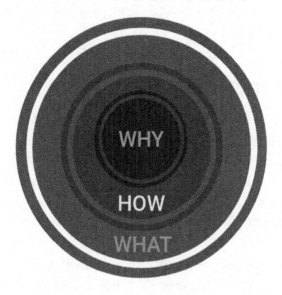

First, there is the neocortex part of our brain that is responsible for rational and analytical thought. This corresponds with the WHAT level of the brain represented by the outermost ring in the circle. Next, there is the limbic brain that is responsible for feelings, like trust and loyalty. The limbic brain is associated with the middle two sections of the circle, which correspond with the HOW and the WHY. In the limbic parts of the brain, there is no capacity for words or language. In this area, decisions are made based on a feeling. Hence, these are often labeled as decisions that are determined by "go with your gut" or "lead with your heart" type of an approach.

The Golden Circle helps explain why we have strong initial "heart reactions" to both people and companies and why it is important to study the elements that will help make that reaction a positive one.

Build YOUR Golden Circle

As you determine what the driving force is in your business, it's important to define several other pieces of the equation. First, and most importantly, WHY do you do what you do? Think about what drives you beyond just a paycheck. Why does your organization exist? What gets you excited to tackle the day? Why does anyone care?

After you nail down your WHY, then the HOW and the WHAT will organically follow along. HOW will you deliver your unique or proprietary process that delivers your product or service? HOW is that different from anyone else's way to doing things? Finally, WHAT is the product or service that your organization provides on a basic level? Is it clearly defined and communicated? Once you hone in on the answers to your WHY, HOW, and WHAT you can enter them in your own Golden Circle and you will begin to see how they work together to present to the neocortex and limbic systems of your future customers and clients.

Now, think through the definitions and determine the WHY, HOW and WHAT in your business. Write them down in a place you'll see and be reminded of them every day.

- WHY does your company exist?

- WHY do you get out of bed in the morning?

- WHY does anyone care?

- HOW do you provide a unique process to add value?

- WHAT product or service does your company or organization provide?

(*Note: A true WHY is not money driven. It is a purpose that goes deeper than just compensation alone. If you've ever heard someone say, "I love what I do so much I'd do it for free!" they are probably saying that because they are motivated by their WHY, not their earnings).

"People Don't Buy WHAT You Do, They Buy WHY You Do It"

As the CEO of your own business, it is critical that you become clear as to why you are in business. It is the main building block upon which you will build. And the reason it is so important is, as Simon Sinek says, "people don't buy WHAT you do, they buy WHY you do it." If YOU aren't clear on why you do what you do, then nobody else can get behind it either.

Here's a personal example. I love helping women and *milpreneurs* build their business while learning to Live, Give, Serve, and Grow. I do this through an encouraging word here, a piece of advice there, and an occasional kick in the pants (all in the spirit of helping others reach their full potential)! But, do you think anyone would value my input if I was not clear about my purpose, or my WHY? There would be no underlying trust, no credibility, no authenticity, and no interest in what I was offering. And, I probably wouldn't have been able to organize a tribe of *milpreneurs* who are out there changing the world!

Let's take a look at an example. While I generally try to eat healthy, I simply can't resist Sugar Shack Coffee & Donuts, my favorite place to grab a treat in Northern Virginia. I think most locals would agree that their handmade cake donuts and white chocolate mochas are amazing. But my true love for the company runs much deeper than just sugary-sweetness. I'm moved by their purpose, their values, and how they make each customer feel.

Let's look at how their HOW and WHAT to see how it fits into the Golden Circle and how that shapes what they do:

- WHAT: Sugar Shack makes donut-related treats and coffee.

- HOW: They hand-roll each donut from scratch and make each cup of coffee individually with fresh ingredients and attention to detail.

Sugar Shack's HOW and WHAT are the nuts and bolts of how they operate. They are the words written on their website, on their signage, and in their store. If Sugar Shack used only these elements in their marketing, the pitch would sound similar to everyone else's and it might look something like this:

We make delicious treats and great coffee.

Not just any kind, but handmade treats and premium coffee, made with fresh ingredients and lots of love.

Want some?

If Sugar Shack went with this basic marketing approach, I seriously doubt it would stand out amongst the Dunkin Donuts and the Krispy Kreme's of the world. But thankfully, the Sugar Shack WHY is deeper than just the nuts and bolts. What I learned from talking with the owner, Rob Krupicka, is that Sugar Shack donuts represent so much more than a simple pastry ring of fresh ingredients. What truly makes them stand out is their WHY.

- WHY: The Sugar Shack brand seeks to build community. It brings people together. It employs people who may not otherwise be employable. It puts a smile on people's faces in an otherwise overworked and stressed out world. It provides people a much-needed treat both physically and emotionally.

You can clearly see this come to life when you look at the photos on the wall of happy local community members eating donuts. You can see in the brochures how the store supports local children's and arts programs. Plus, you can see it in the cute t-shirts that customers are proudly wearing that say,

"Donut know what I'd do without you." Sugar Shack's WHY oozes from every possible corner of their donut shop.

As you aim to appeal to customers, when you start with WHY, it helps customers feel the reason for your existence as a business, not just the features and benefits of WHAT and HOW it works. Using WHY as the starting point, Sugar Shack's marketing might look like this:

> *If you are too busy, too stressed, and looking for a tasty treat to feed your soul, bring your tribe together and put a smile on your face, then Sugar Shack is your place.*
>
> *We make delicious treats and great coffee.*
>
> *Not just any kind, but one-of-a-kind handmade treats and the highest-quality premium coffee made with fresh ingredients and lots of love.*
>
> *Want some?*

The *HOW* Should Align With *WHY*

Once you have clearly determined WHY you're in business, then the HOW and the WHAT should follow (in that order) with a strong belief in what you will do, with honest authenticity, and with a sense of trust that your customers can count on.

Belief is Paramount

I have never been more inspired by a story of belief than that of military spouses, Lisa Bradley and Cameron Cruse, as they formed their company, R. Riveter. Their inspiration was built on their passionate belief in the idea that military spouses could make a difference and empower one another through business.

R. Riveter, which sells elegant handbags from upcycled military uniforms, believed there was a way to have mobile and flexible careers that military spouses could take with them. To do that, they built their business plan around the concept that every product would be hand-crafted and assembled by military spouses employed by R. Riveter. These "Riveters," who could live anywhere in the country, would sew the pieces and parts required to build a handbag and then send all their work to one location to complete the bags.

It is important to note that R. Riveter could have easily resorted to a traditional assembly method where bags were sewn together in a production line in a warehouse. It might have been cheaper and easier. But they chose their process of HOW: using uniforms that would be carefully assembled by military spouses employed by the company, because it better aligned with their WHY. And it felt like it fit.

Their start-up was definitely a labor of love that came with many ups and downs, both financially and emotionally. The founders' belief in their concept and their mission to employ military spouses fueled their fire through every phase, good and bad. Their first big break came in 2014 when they ran a very successful Kickstarter crowdsourcing campaign that allowed them to push their business up a notch with additional funding.

Less than two years later, they were fortunate enough to gain an invitation to the ABC hit show, "Shark Tank" and gain a deal with the Dallas Mavericks' owner, Mark Cuban. In just a year since the show aired, the company has grown immensely and currently employs thirty local employees and twenty-seven Independent Contractor "Riveters" across the nation.

Today, R. Riveter has grown so much larger than anyone ever conceived it would in the early days. It is great proof that understanding your deep-seated purpose, or WHY, is all you need to get a strong start in business. Then the HOW should naturally follow and feel good. As Lisa Bradley says, "When you grow a business it takes on a life of its own—under your guidance. Knowing that the pains and pleasures are a product of our own decisions and our creation is the most rewarding career experience I can imagine."

The R. Riveter founders don't see their hard work as something that is purely measured in numbers and profit. For the two of them, the company was successful the moment it revealed to them that "being fulfilled as a military spouse isn't about that dream job or title to define who you are. R. Riveter has taught us that you can do so much in this world and have a huge impact on people's lives."

Authenticity is Important

Authenticity is when the Golden Circle of a businessess's WHAT, HOW, and WHY are in perfect alignment and people can sense it. While interviewing other successful entrepreneurs, the one common thread I have heard over and over again is the fact that authenticity had a part to play in the way their customers received their perceived mission. People can sniff out an insincere business offer, and they tend to find more value in those that feel genuine and authentic.

If you think of the US military as a brand, authenticity is what they do better than anyone else on the planet. Most service members are drawn to and join the military because they have a deep desire to serve. We've all heard a token story of a person who left a comfortable life to join the ranks of their fellow service members because they were moved by a specific war or another cause that the US military was fighting for. That kind of commitment is not something you can fake. It takes an honest, patriotic, and service-driven individual. And in a world that can get very messy with media, business, and politics, Americans know that they can always count on the commitment, strength, and service of the US military.

This authenticity, combined with a WHY that centers on serving others, is exactly what makes people in the military community great entrepreneurs. As service members, they are reminded often to embrace the concepts of "integrity first," "service before self," and "excellence in all we do." And they become a way of life. Then as military entrepreneurs, the same concepts become the building blocks of their business. Service is interwoven into everything they do. It is second nature to work hard, please customers, give a great experience, and endure delayed gratification through the toils of building the business. This is how they are trained and what a service member has practiced through years of serving his or her country. In the end, this kind of authentic entrepreneurship is something we can all learn from and spread.

Begin With WHY

To gain a desirable sense of authenticity, I found that the most business owners, like dedicated patriots, started with WHY and organically built their WHAT and HOW. In an authentically WHY-centered business, money, fame and success are second to the intense desire to fulfill a company or an entrepreneur's WHY. Yet, the irony is that many times while laser-focused on achieving a WHY, an eager entrepreneur may find their way to big fame and fortune as a by-product.

One business story that illustrates this concept is that of Jen Robbins and *Predominantly Paleo*. Jen is a fellow military spouse who had a fairly uneventful health history, until she turned twenty-six and a mysterious chronic illness set in. Between panic attacks, autoimmune disease, a Lyme scare, and a myriad of other diagnoses, Jen's body was literally giving up on her. Her illness landed her in a scary state where she was left sick and housebound for months at a time. I remember visiting with her after the birth of her third child and listening to her describe rough days where she was literally bound to her bed due to incapacitating vertigo and other gut issues that made carrying her baby, driving her other two kids to school, or attending military events nearly impossible.

But somehow the rock-bottom moments were what gave Jen the mental resolve to find the solution no doctor could provide her. That's when she changed her diet and began her journey to recovery. Jen says, "In this discovery and quest for natural healing, I realized that if I wanted to heal, I would need to be the key player in my wellness. Even doctors with the best intentions could not care for me on a molecular level, only I could do that."

So, she started by taking out gluten from her diet and eating grain free. Then she eliminated dairy and replaced it with smarter and cleaner food choices and began teaching herself to cook simple, nutrition-filled meals that would begin her incredible recovery. As her health began to rebound Jen started sharing her discoveries in her blog, *Predominantly Paleo*, and eventually through her cookbooks and her spin-off bread company, Legit Bread.

But it all started from her simple WHY. As she states on her website, "My goal is to share my story, share my journey, and share my recipes in hopes that others who are struggling may find life again as well."

What's so impressive about her story is that Jen really had no intentions of becoming an Amazon best-seller with her cookbooks or a big-time CEO. When she began blogging, she was merely using her voice and her discoveries as a way to reach out and help other sick people find a ray of hope through her struggles.

As I recently attended one of Jen's book signings in Philadelphia, it was breathtaking to watch her *Predominantly Paleo* fans come up to her and thank her for changing their health and, in some cases, for changing their lives. It was obvious that her followers understood WHY she devotes herself to her work. She keeps this at the forefront of everything she does, and you can feel her passion to help sick people come through. For a WHY-centered CEO, that's all the payment needed. Jen is an awesome example of achieving her authentic why and allowing the success to follow.

Trust

What happens when you believe in your WHY and authentically align your WHAT and HOW is that you build trust in your customer base. And with trust comes brand loyalty and a committed following. The great part is that your loyal followers don't have to be incentivized, convinced or persuaded to support your cause. They naturally follow because they believe so deeply in your mission!

How Do I Find My WHY?

When you break down your WHY into its simplest form, you are looking to define the population you will serve with your product or service. Apple serves a population who wants to "challenge the status quo" and look at the world through a different lens. R. Riveter put their business in motion to prove to military spouses that there WAS a portable work solution to the unemployment problem for military spouses. Jen Robins started her *Predominantly Paleo* blog to help educate and inspire other people suffering from chronic illness to heal themselves with healthy food choices. *Mission*: Milpreneur seeks to educate those who want to build businesses using the lessons learned from military life. Now let's hone in on yours. In order to clearly find *your* WHY, follow these helpful steps:

Top 5 Ways to Discover Your WHY:

1.   Make a List of Your Life's Self-Defining Activities

Each of us has labels we have gathered through life. Artist, athlete, actor, Mom, sorority sister, choir member, Zumba instructor, etc, etc. In defining the specific population you will serve, ask yourself these three questions and your WHY will begin to emerge:

1. What groups were you a part of that you identify with?

- E.g., College volleyball team, Women's Air Force Officer Group, book club, MOPS, Running Club

2. Where have you worked?

- E.g., Pool lifeguard, Air Force, golf course, decorating business, business coach

3. What makes you who you are?

- E.g., Service driven, part of something bigger than me, tough but feminine military gal

This last question is a great one to ask yourself and may lead to a tweaking of your WHY statement as well. For me, this revelation did not come until after almost eighteen months in business. I knew I wasn't in business for the money. But it took a while for me to recognize a sense of service within my career was really important to me and after leaving the military I lacked that. Having made this discovery, today my business fills that role for me. Serving and giving have become a huge part of my entrepreneurial journey because of my WHY.

2. Re-engage With the Population You Want to Serve

On the way to fulfilling your WHY, find groups related to the population you want to serve and genuinely get to know people. Then learn the major topics of conversation taking place within this population and how you can add value. Connect with other groups related to your population on social media (LinkedIn, Twitter, and Facebook) and begin conversations. Find ways to expand your network to more related groups.

When I first moved to the Washington, DC area and was trying to get my business off the ground, I didn't have any local contacts or connections. I was in search of where to begin, so I simply started attending any job-related fair for military spouses and made a point to meet people. That eventually led me to a networking organization where I was introduced to several of my future business partners.

Once you define who it is you want to work with and for, immerse yourself in getting to know them, find out what they need and want in life, and make it a point to interact enough to ensure your WHY, HOW, and WHAT make sense for them.

3. Become the Go-to Expert

As a young Lieutenant in the Air Force, my job was to manage a bunch of intense and foul-mouthed airplane mechanics who were not much younger than I was. I found myself in many situations where I was standing in front of 250 of these young maintenance troops and I needed to say just the right thing to gain their respect and get them to follow my lead. This could have been very intimidating, given that I was so young and inexperienced in the field of aircraft maintenance. I could have easily let my fears get the better of me. But a wise mentor of mine once told me that I didn't need to know every aspect of the aircraft or the tools or the lingo to be respected. I just needed to be an expert in something. I have carried that advice with me ever since and I think it applies to the business world too.

You should strive to become the resident expert within your field. Find out what your target market is lacking with the current options available to them. What problems do they have to overcome? What is their biggest need? Where can you provide value with your experience or skill? How can you bring a unique perspective to their existing frustrations? How can you make a better product or service?

Once you gain a position as an industry leader in a specific area of need, you create demand for your services, and you naturally will build a set of fans that can't help but follow your lead.

4. Find People Who Value What You Do

As your WHY becomes clear and you build the HOW and the WHAT around YOUR Golden Circle, make sure you keep in mind that you are looking to attract people who share similar values and are motivated by similar goals. Hire people who share passions that connect with your WHY, not just because they have an impressive work history or stellar resume. Choose people who fit with your organization and who have potential to grow and expand within the context of your WHY. Your work environment should inspire your colleagues to produce their very best because they are invested in the mindset of what you're trying to achieve. Ironically, it doesn't take big paychecks or fancy promises to attract the right people. They will be drawn to what you stand for and WHY you exist.

5. Practice and Gain Confidence

Now that you've determined your WHY and your specific target market, GET BUSY! You know your own customer's needs better than anyone, so confidently attack your work with the belief that you are the best one to talk to this particular population of people. Challenge yourself to push the limits of your comfort zone and keep looking for new ways to grow. Once you get to the point where you are comfortable, think of other ways you can strengthen your area of expertise.

Chapter 4

Five Easy Business Options to Get Started

A s I began to realize the amazing benefits of using my military experience to my advantage in business, I started to notice trends within the military entrepreneur scene. I learned that a lot of the success stories were centered on similar types of flexible and portable businesses.

Now, whether you are drawn to the portable business ideas I'm about to share, you have other amazing ideas already in the works, or you are looking for an idea to spark your imagination, here are a few characteristics of business models that are compatible with military life.

Top Business Models Compatible with Military Lifestyle:

*1. They are **portable** so they can operate in any location in any country*

*2. They have a relatively **low startup cost***

*3. They require little to **no experience***

*4. They are **flexible** enough to work around deployments, kids' school schedules, military unit requirements, and location changes*

*5. They give business owners full **autonomy** to scale as big as they want*

All right, so how can you get started?

With these characteristics in mind, let's explore five easy business options that work really well for military spouses wanting to start a business. Even if these businesses don't appeal to you at first, I recommend reading this entire section. You will discover useful business and productivity tips, be amazed at the resilient lives of our *Milpreneur* tribe, and be inspired by stories of overcoming the odds to live, give, serve, and grow.

Top 5 Portable Business Options:

1. Blogging

Having watched military entrepreneurs closely for the past 10 years, the most popular option I've seen is to start a blog. Now, if you're like me, I initially thought blogging was just a place to write down thoughts and share your opinions on a topic (and there are definitely plenty of hobby bloggers out there that do just that). But believe it or not, blogging can also be a wildly lucrative business.

To create business around a blog, a blogger should pick an area of expertise, or niche, in which they can publish content that provides value to their readers. If their content strikes a chord and creates a large demand they can then monetize their blogging through multiple income streams.

Remember Jen Robins from Chapter 3? Her blog was never intended to be a business when she started it in 2013. In fact, she didn't "even know what blogging was" when she began. Rather, her reason for starting initially was to have an online location to store her Paleo recipes so that she could find them again. She would catalog them with pictures so she could find them and share them with friends and family members. Occasionally, Jen would notice that a recipe would get "shared" on Pinterest and she would wonder how in the world people had found her site. She would never know if anyone was sharing her content on Facebook or Twitter because she, herself, wasn't even on those platforms yet. But even without accounts on those platforms, her content was picking up popularity.

After a year, Jen decided to make her hobby something more formal and she started a social media page, titled *Predominantly Paleo.* Looking back, she claims that the first version of her site was "kind of embarrassing." But she didn't let that stop her. She decided a cookbook was in order and went straight to pitching publishers for what would later, after several refusals and failed attempts, become her first book, *Down South Paleo.* The book was a hit and she went on to publish three more books within the next couple years.

Jen's biggest piece of advice is, "Don't ignore your entrepreneurial spirit." She encourages anyone who feels like they have something valuable to contribute to the world to start a blog. It's something anyone can do around a nine-to-five job, or to replace one. Even housebound and with poor health, she was able to make it work, and she wants that to be an inspiration to others that they can do the same. Even if your first attempts aren't perfect and fail, "don't believe that's the end of your story." Pick up and try again. As she says, "Everyone deserves the ability to plant your dream and grow it. Don't let any failure or anyone stop you."

Like Jen, Maureen Dougherty didn't have a master plan to create a money-making blog either. As a military spouse living overseas, she started her blog to be able to communicate with her family back home in the US. Given her love of handbags and cute shoes, a lot of her blog content also included information about "where to get a look" or "what was on sale."

In 2013, as Maureen and her Air Force fighter-pilot husband, Curt, relocated back to the States and added a child to the family, Maureen began looking for alternative ways to work and decided that blogging about her love of fashion could be the answer.

Given that she is a Pennsylvania native, Maureen named the blog *The Northeast Girl* and began sharing styled photographs of herself wearing her J.Crew-inspired, easy-going looks. She gained a strong following of middle-class moms and within several years, she held a good piece of market share in the girl-next-door fashion blogging market. As a smart business owner, Maureen continued to expand her brand by adding in other streams of income, to include sponsored content, cross-promotions with other bloggers and related beauty items.

Both of these successful *milpreneur* bloggers attribute their success to staying authentic to their followers and not being swayed by offers from stores or advertisers that wouldn't jive with their brand ideals. Maureen says, "stay true to yourself. In a world that's filled with carbon copies, the only way you can be sure to stand out in the crowd is just to be you!" Here are some other helpful tips to follow when starting a blog:

Tips to Start or Grow a Blog:

1. Find your angle

It is wise to choose a blog theme that people can easily understand and follow. Start with a niche that is unique to you. Get really good at what you know within your niche and remain focused. If you're going to be a fashion blogger, stick to fashion. If you want to build a food blog, stick to just food. With so many influences in today's society, it can be easy to get distracted and lose your original focus. Once you've established yourself with your readers and you've gained their trust, then you may see opportunities to branch out. But building trust with your readers is definitely a key piece to a strong start. Jen says, "If you don't earn trust, you're not building a foundation that can grow."

2. Find a blog name that clearly states what you're doing

The name of your blog is one of the most enjoyable elements of starting up. It can be fun. It can be clever. It can be a play on words. Or it can plainly state the obvious. But no matter what approach you take to picking your blog name, make sure that it clearly explains the purpose of your blog.

Jen stumbled upon a great name with *Predominantly Paleo*, even though she initially thought that it would be a placeholder. Fortunately, she decided not to change it when she realized that people were finding her on the Internet because of the clear understanding of the blog's purpose in her blog name. Jen cautions bloggers from choosing a family or child's name because something so specific can hinder the organic reach and searchability of your blog. Maureen appeals to the preppy and classic fashion found in the Northeast. Hence, she named her blog the *Northeast Girl*. Once you decide on a name for your blog, go ahead and purchase the domain name.

3. Self-host your blog

Jen's original blog was hosted on www.blogger.com, which is a site that provides an easy way for novice bloggers to get their blog out onto the Internet. But, the downside is that bloggers using this service do not own the intellectual property they create and publish on the www.blogger.com platform. Once Jen wanted to transition *Predominantly Paleo* from a convenient place to host recipes to a full-blown monetized blog, it required that she seek out her own self-hosted blog site. One easy place to self-host is on www.wordpress.com. Other popular options include www.squarespace.com and www.tumblr.com. Most of these reputable blog hosting sites are affordable and allow you to own your own content, in case you should want to reuse the information elsewhere in the future. One thing people love about starting a blog is that it is so affordable. Both Jen and Maureen launched their blogs successfully for less than $100/ month in hosting fees.

4. Post new blog content on a regular schedule

Another key piece to a blog that gets a strong start is to have the blog peppered with enough content to allow a person the chance to get lost in multiple interesting pieces of content. To do that you need to think ahead. Jen suggests that it's a good idea to make a list of 100+ ideas of good content you could publish up front. In her case, she called friends and asked them what were one hundred different Paleo recipes they would want to eat if she could make them? That became the fodder for her first set of posts. For new bloggers, Jen says write blog posts on 10-20 useful topics before you announce your blog to anyone. When writing the posts, make sure they are three hundred words or more so they have a chance to get noticed via search engine optimization (SEO).

Once your blog is published, keep putting out content at regularly scheduled intervals so your readers can become accustomed on when to look for new posts. Maureen says if you want to grow your blog, "Treat it like it's a job. Set a schedule, develop a routine and be as consistent as possible." Then, leverage posts by sharing them on as many social media sites as possible. The best posts are engaging, funny, or informative so feel free to let your personality show through, which will keep people coming back!

5. Include affiliate links, ads, and giveaways to monetize your blog

There are several strategies that Jen has successfully used to monetize her blog. The first is to add affiliate links into organic content wherever it makes sense. In a nutshell, an affiliate link is a specific URL that links to an affiliate company or store that sells the item being highlighted. In most affiliate programs, advertisers use affiliate links to record the traffic that is sent to the advertiser's website.

In the case of a blog, the blogger mentions their favorite products or services and includes their affiliate link when they mention them. If any of their readers click on the link or makes a purchase, the blogger is rewarded with a small fee or percentage of the sale. In the military world, recommendations are the lifeblood of how we find our favorite vendors, so this is a very valuable tool to utilize with your blog. Maureen says, "know your worth, network with fellow influencers, and pitch ideas to your favorite brands so you can collaborate and cross promote."

The most popular affiliate program today is with Amazon.com, because they sell such a wide range of products that appeal to almost any kind of blogger. Amazon pays between 4-15% for their affiliate sales. Other popular options are: Commission Junction, LinkShare, and Shareasale. In the fashion department, popular choices are Shopstyle and RewardStyle.

Ads are another way to leverage your blog to make money. Jen describes blogs as "prime real estate" and as they gain a following, their value goes up. Therefore, people will pay an associated cost to advertise on the blog's "beachfront real estate." Companies like Media Brand and Ad Thrive are good ones to look at for possible advertising opportunities.

Finally, giveaways can also be a valuable strategy for growing and monetizing your blog. There are several ways you can do this. In the beginning, you can use a purchased giveaway item to draw in readers by asking them each to: "Enter to win by tagging two friends and you could win. But if you can't wait, here is the (affiliate) link to purchase your own today!" Once your blog has grown, you can partner with brands that have an advertising budget and highlight their product for an associated fee.

Believe that if you build it, they will come

Both Jen and Maureen agree that you have to commit to your blog for the long term. No business magically grows overnight and your blog won't either, so mentally commit for an extended period of time. Find a way to truly enjoy the process and not just evaluate your growth based solely on earnings. Remember that failure is a huge part of your growth and have fun!!

2. Photography

With the popularity of the DSLR camera, smartphones, and camera technology, the number of photography businesses has exploded! Additionally, with more options for how and where to print pictures and easy access to creative photo editing software and apps, a business that used to be hard to learn and expensive to maintain has become possible for the amateur photographer.

Our family has moved (or PCS'd as we call it in the military) five times within the last ten years, and at each location I chronicle our time there with family pictures. Almost *all* of the photographers we've used in that time frame were military spouse entrepreneurs, *milpreneurs*.

Military spouse, Courtney Slazinik, took the idea of marketing photography skills even one step further and decided to teach other novice photographers how to use their cameras. As a new mom with a DSLR camera, she learned how to use the camera from another friend who was willing to show her. From there, she participated in a project called Project 365, where she took one picture per day for an entire year. This project gave her plenty of opportunity to practice what she had learned.

At this point, Courtney was living in Japan and began watching other bloggers online to learn from them. She realized that they were monetizing their blogs with advertising and figured she could do the same. She remembers thinking, "I can make six hundred dollars a month. This is going to be amazing!"

So, in 2010, she started Click It Up A Notch, where she set out to help people unlock the power of their DSLR cameras and take better pictures of the day-to-day love and laughter in their lives. Courtney started her business without a huge expectation that it would transform into what it has today, but she knew it would fill her professional cup and provide her the recognition and fulfillment that she was craving as a stay-at-home mom.

Thankfully, Courtney had a long-range vision when she began, thanks to the advice of others. She "had always heard that it takes three years to get anything off the ground." And quite honestly, she didn't really set out to build a business at first. Upon doing her initial research, she noticed that there were a lot of established photography teachers in the market, so Courtney decided to take a different approach and teach people AS she learned.

She liked the idea that her blog would be a very "real" place for moms to go learn from another mom just like them. Her philosophy was that, "I was not in a place to be an expert. So I just wanted to show people that we could figure it out together." Since Courtney was juggling three young kids, she embraced the fact that life was busy, her house could be messy, but she could still take her readers along on her journey.

Adam Palmer also used the photography platform to create his successful *milpreneur* business called 9for9 Media. Only unlike Courtney, Adam's business development happened mostly on the hour-long commute to and from work, and while on leave status, since Adam is still an active-duty officer for the Air Force.

When he hit the age of thirty, Adam didn't have an overwhelming sense of satisfaction for where his career was headed. He was hungry to find a way to significantly add value to another venture. As luck would have it, he bought a t-shirt from a competitive power lifter in 2014 and was sorely disappointed in the quality. So he volunteered his services to help revamp the t-shirt operation. Along the way, the two became friends and Adam learned that there was a giant need for high-quality professional photography at powerlifting meets. Thus, his business idea was born.

To get some experience, Adam shadowed photographers with *CrossFit Media* who were willing to mentor him and who taught him some of the things he needed to know. Adam had to work for free in those early days taking anything and everything (including wedding photos), but he learned how to produce some awesome content. With some experience under his belt, Adam built a company that would provide still photos and video of power lifters for either personal, promotional or professional purposes. He officially began in 2016.

In the beginning, there were some bumps on Adam's road to success. He admits that he had to learn the hard way on several jobs where he lost money by placing trust in the wrong people. But as he says, "each micro-loss is important" and taught him useful lessons for the future. What Adam did right was focus a lot of time and attention on his social media content and consistently offering high-quality content, which resulted in meteoric growth in the company's followership.

As an active-duty officer, Adam has to take his military leave to attend any his business events. Due to his limited time, he has been forced to hire subcontractors and be very efficient with his process. Despite the late nights and working commutes (his wife drives them to work), Adam says it has "helped improve his mindset as an officer too," because he can pull the practical lessons he is learning from his business back into his military job.

Now that 9for9 Media has hit its stride, Adam uses his large online audience to help drive positive messages about the powerlifting sport. He photographs drug-free lifting events only, and he recently used some clever April Fools photography to raise important questions about the extent to which provocative photography should be allowed in the sport.

Adam says he will continue to use his business to achieve his personal WHY, which is to advance the sport of power lifting! He has plenty of ideas for where to take his brand in the future and he is excited to see how he can help the sport grow. The passion in his voice is undeniable when he says, "Now I get people coming up to me at meets that tell me my photos inspired them to start lifting—that's what I love...it's like, *mission accomplished!*"

Check out Courtney and Adam's tips for starting a photography-related business.

Tips to Start a Photography Business:

1. Start an email list

Courtney encourages every entrepreneur to start an email list. The second you start a website you should start collecting emails from your potential customers. Not only does it help you with your sales, but more importantly, it gives you a way to reach out to them each week to provide value and exclusive content. No one wants to join another newsletter, so don't call it that. Instead make it your VIP list or some other clever name. It helps people to feel like they are a part of a family. Plus, people are more likely to convert into a customer if they are on your email list and get regular communications from you. If you want people to join your list, give them a good reason to join it. Just like Jen Robins suggested in her tips, Courtney also agrees that a giveaway or freebie of some kind is a powerful tool, even if it's a downloadable PDF or a coupon code. Adam adds that when you have a robust email list you can easily provide your customers with up-to-date information on new products or services and you can keep them informed of status changes to orders or company status.

2. Provide value

Courtney and Adam both agree that providing value should be one of your top priorities as an entrepreneur. As Adam says, "your brand and your word are everything, so always strive to produce high-quality content." Yes, you started a business and you want to make money, but ultimately you also want to help people. Your product is able to help people but you also need to provide value in your content in order to truly make an impact. Content marketing is one of the most powerful marketing tools you have at your disposal. Each week write a blog post or email your list with some valuable information. Adam started by posting to Instagram with his photo content at least one time per day. He attributes his consistency to their fast growth. So be consistent. The idea is to give and give and give before you ask for anything in return. Resist the urge to ask for a sale if you haven't provided any value.

3. Build a community for your tribe

Finally, Courtney has proven the power of a strong following and sense of community. She says, "If you have an email list and are providing value then you are building a community." People want to feel like they are a part of something special. They want to be a part of a tribe. A tribe that you lead. Make sure you offer special value or discounts to your treasured community. This is how you get people to organically want to share about your business with their friends. And that's when you will unlock bigger growth.

3.   Social Commerce

Blogger, business expert, and best-selling author Seth Godin says in his book *Permission Marketing,* "You can use social media to turn strangers into friends, friends into customers and customers into salespeople."

With the rise in social media and the decline of brick and mortar stores, the e- or social commerce market has exploded with vendors marketing their products through the viral power of online connections.

I was introduced to this new trend in social commerce in 2009 from my childhood friend and financial advisor, Jamie Petersen. As someone with experience in looking for companies with upside potential, she saw a big future in an up and coming skincare company. She told me it was "not what I thought," but rather it was a social commerce company started by reputable doctors. They provided premium anti-aging skincare and tools via consultants who used word of mouth techniques on social media. This definitely caught my attention.

Although my initial reaction was to lump this into the same category as the traditional at-home businesses of my childhood, I could sense that there was an element to this that was much more cutting edge and trendsetting than it may have seemed at first. As I learned more, I realized it was an amazing fit for military spouses because of the portability, low investment, and team building elements, so I jumped in and began sharing it amongst my military friends.

The idea took off like wildfire, and within six months I had collaborated with eight amazing women to begin building our initial dream team. Within eighteen months, we had grown to a team size of a few hundred consultants and our annual sales production was in the ballpark of 1.5 million dollars. Six years into the business, our growth has clearly proven the viability and insane potential of this business model. Today, we have over nine thousand consultants on our team and estimates for 2017 show that we will do over eighteen million dollars in sales this year.

But the best part I discovered about starting my own social commerce business is the fact that I get to work alongside a team of other independent business owners. Each of us has the autonomy to build our own unique brand and business, but we can still come together and collaborate on how to grow together, how to help one another, and how to continuously build a new generation of leaders to keep our brand moving full steam ahead into new global markets.

Read on to some important tips to start a social commerce business.

Tips to Start a Social Commerce Business:

1. Build around your passion

As we discussed in Chapter 3, no business remains strong if there isn't a strong WHY to drive an entrepreneur when the going gets tough. Yet, a lot of people forget to take the proper time to identify their WHY before they get busy with the details of their WHAT and HOW. Take enough time to clearly define

WHY you started your business and how your WHY will further your passions in life. When the hard days hit, and they most certainly will, you will use your WHY as a "reset button" to remind you what was driving you in the first place. Make sure that as you build a team of business owners that you take the time to coach them through their WHYs as well. When you have a team running towards their passion, it doesn't matter what the product is, you will most definitely succeed!

Micaela Brancato, both an Air National Guard officer and *milpreneur* wanted to create a way she could continue serving her sisters and brothers in arms even after her impending retirement from the military. She and her pilot husband, Matt, lost several friends to service-related incidents over a short time span and felt led to help. They immediately jumped in to help do everything they could to care for the widows left behind. When Matt and Micaela began their social commerce business they realized they could connect the two efforts. Building a retreat center for widows of service members became their WHY and their motivation to continue growing their business when time was short, working a side gig wasn't always convenient, and military commitments took priority. Without this WHY, it might have been easy for them to give up during the tough times. But with consistent growth and effort and by keeping their eye on their WHY they were able to open Holbrook Farms Retreat Center five years ahead of their original schedule. Holbrook Farms provides a wonderful all-expenses paid week of lake activities, yoga and fellowship for military widows on their beautiful and serene property in Minnesota each summer.

2. Design a business that you love

The beautiful thing about this business model is that you get to call all the shots yourself. Nobody can tell you what hours you want to work, who you choose to partner with, and in what regions or cities you decide to really dig in and grow teams. So, build it in a manner that is most beneficial to your schedule, your family, and your desires.

Milpreneur, veteran, and former ER nurse Shannon Burke moved nineteen times in thirty years as a military spouse. She was extremely tired of finding and leaving nursing jobs with twelve-hour shifts that didn't always pay well and left her kids to latchkey status. So when she started her business, she made it a point to build her business hours around her boys' baseball practices, her husband's military functions, and her own love of CrossFit. Her transition to *milpreneurism* has made a world of difference to her family and to her overall happiness.

3. Be consistent

If there is one secret to my team's growth it is that we put the military work ethic into action and remain very committed and consistent to activity in our businesses. Even though we may not have had the flashiest success out of the gate or held the highest records for sales, you couldn't find a team more diligent and more disciplined in their approach to business.

One place I've seen this to be true is the daily work routines and habits. Many of my military business partners are experts at holding themselves to a work routine, day in and day out. Like so many military spouses, I learned the dire importance of a routine when I was left to function as a single parent during my husband's deployments. Without a routine, I might have lost my marbles.

The same goes for business. A consistent and reliable daily approach to your business provides you the peace and calm needed to see a business plan through to the end. Little steps forward may not always seem like big progress at the time, but they add up. Strive to set up a consistent daily plan of action and form good habits from the beginning.

When you put this consistent military work ethic together with long range vision, resilience, and selflessness, it will be your winning combo!

4. Be coachable and keep learning

Finally, be coachable and continue to be a student of the business. This takes a certain amount of humility and an understanding that you can never master every aspect of the business. You can continually find new ways to keep improving. The best way to learn is to watch those who have gone before you. Learn from their mistakes. Be open to their feedback. Watch their techniques and practice what they teach you. Put your own spin on the lessons they provide and then step into your own leadership shoes to teach the entrepreneurs behind you in the same way.

4.   Product or Service

Most businesses start by finding a solution to a problem with a product or service. Since finding solutions is one of the staples of military training, this category of business is plentiful with great product solutions. If you have watched the ABC hit show *Shark Tank* in the past several years, there have been military entrepreneurs with energy drinks, military-inspired jewelry, dog treats, and home organizing systems. It seems that there is no end to the clever product solutions that arise from military minds.

I was particularly inspired by Bridget Platt's story. Bridget is a military spouse who learned just ten days after her first child was born that her husband, a pilot in the military, would be deployed for seven months. As abrupt and disappointing as this news was, like most military spouses, Bridget took it in stride and took a calm, cool, and collected approach to easing herself and her newborn into the change. She immediately started to research what children's books were available to explain the deployment process to small children.

As she searched, she found that the options were anything but positive. In fact, a lot of the options available were surprisingly negative. So, Bridget took it upon herself to write her daughter "her own story" that included bright colors, a story of strength about a military family, and an ending that wasn't sad like all the others. In 2012, that story went on to be the start of her children's book company, Daddy's Deployed. The company's mission is to customize books for children to help them understand what to expect when Mommy or Daddy is told they will be deploying or moving to a new assignment location. The books can be customized for one child or for a whole family of children so they truly feel a part of the story.

Bridget's success has allowed her family to have a lot of options they wouldn't have otherwise had without her business. Since the launch of her business, her husband retired from the Marines and transitioned to the civilian world. They have added another child to their family as well. All in all, the business has been an empowering endeavor for the entire family. Check out Bridget's tips for launching your retail product.

Tips for Launching a Retail Product:

1. Late nights and early mornings

Entrepreneurship is hard work. There is no question about that. Bridget's advice for the budding entrepreneur who is trying to launch a product is that in order to juggle family and business, you just have to accept that there will be some late nights and early mornings. It can be hard to focus during the commotion of the day with family. Some quiet hours before they wake up or after they go to bed are when some of the best work gets done.

2. Use your resources

Bridget was the master of finding a plethora of resources
available to her through programs like Patriot Boot Camp,
VWISE (an extension of Syracuse University), and *Inc.
Magazine*'s Military Entrepreneur Program. Become educated
on the resources available in your area and online. Find a
great mentor to help you navigate the unknown and then turn
around and provide those services to others as well.

3. Leverage social media

When Bridget started Daddy's Deployed, she had a good
understanding of how she could leverage the power of social
media to help perpetuate her books. She immediately began to
cultivate a following on her Facebook page, which grew quickly,
and she eventually handed it over to another military spouse
run company, Pressed Branding.

4. Make a connection with your customers

There is no doubt that there will be ups and downs in any
entrepreneur's journey. However, the WHY that keeps a person
focused and driven is essential to long-term success. Bridget
finds that WHY in the relationships she gets to form with
each family that buys her personalized books. Whether it is
through the homecoming pictures she gets to enjoy, pictures of
the family reading together, or stories of how the books have
helped ease the burden of a deployment, she knows her product
is making a true difference in the lives of those who order it.

5. Online Courses

Like social commerce, online learning and courses are one of
the fastest growing industries in today's business landscape.
The great thing about them is that they can complement a
blog or a website following and if you provide valuable content
that is in high enough demand, they can be a healthy source
of revenue for a short span of time. Course content can also be
repeated multiple times throughout a year, so it builds some
residual income.

One of my favorite online course providers is Marie Forleo
who teaches a highly sought after business start-up training
course simply named, "B School." Marie is also a video blogger
with a weekly video segment called Marie TV that has grown
immensely in its popularity since debuting in 2012 because of
its valuable and funny business advice. One thing I love about
Forleo's B School, is that they provide scholarships every year
to cover the cost of tuition to B School and it is common to
find at least one *milpreneur* in the list of scholarship winners
each year.

Courtney Slazinik was a student of the B School and she put
what she learned about entrepreneurism to work in the early
days of Click It Up A Notch. Specifically, when it comes to
online courses, she was able to put her expertise in motion
and build several helpful and lucrative courses for moms
who wanted to learn specific strategies for using their DSLR
camera. Once Courtney perfected the course content, length of

course, and price, she was able to build up interest with affiliate connections that would drive traffic her way.

So, whether your online course is a stand-alone business or a compliment to a successful blog or website, there is huge value in pursuing online courses as a reliable revenue source. Also, be aware that if you feel overwhelmed at the thought of writing and filming your own course content, there are plenty of aspiring copywriters and videographers that will be willing to help you craft your course. Who knows? You may even be able to trade them your product or service as payment for their help!

Tips to Starting Your On-line Courses:

1. Fulfill a need with your content

Don't just start a course to make money. Rather, find a gap in what is currently offered and find a way to fill the need for information with your course. If you're solving someone's problems, you will likely attract a large organic population and the money should follow. Ask yourself, "Who will take this course?" and "What are my learning objectives?" Then, reverse engineer your content to make sure you hit the main objectives that your ideal customer desires.

2. Use interactive methods

Because we are in fast-paced, technology-driven society, people's attention spans are short and getting shorter. In fact, in a study done by Microsoft, they found that since the year 2000 (when mobile devices gained popularity), the average attention span dropped from twelve seconds to eight seconds. That means we have shorter attention spans than a goldfish. Therefore, you will want to pay extra-special attention to how you are keeping your students engaged in course content. Things like video, worksheets, online forums, and accountability groups can be good ways to maintain interest and commitment.

3. Bring energy to your content[19]

After years of public speaking, I can tell you that energy is the most important ingredient when it comes to making a lasting impression on your audience. If you clearly present your content, give your audience relevant ways to apply the knowledge, AND weave high energy throughout, they will be much more likely to remember what you taught them. The saying goes that people "won't remember what you say, but they'll never forget the way you make them feel." That's what you want your course participants to get; a memorable and lasting experience that is worth sharing with others.

In an overwhelming sea of choices when it comes to business start-ups, my hope is that this review of the five most common business models for military entrepreneurs will spark an idea of what is possible. These business models work really well for military families because they are easy, portable, affordable, flexible, and afford you lots of autonomy to be the CEO you want. Now it's just a matter of finding the one that works best for you.

Chapter 5

What Holds Us Back?

I f there is one thing that *always* accompanies a good business start-up, it's a robust list of fears. Whether the fears make sense or not, once you have declared your business idea they inevitably emerge. As well-known author Stephen King once said, "The scariest part is just before you start." Isn't that the truth? Haven't we all had a great business idea that has popped into our head at some point or another? But then what happens? The ugly fears begin to surface: Money. Time. Failure. What people will think.

These are silent killers of some of the world's most amazing ideas.

In working with thousands of entrepreneurs, I've never met one who hasn't had their own personal hang-ups with a set of fears. I can only imagine all the amazing businesses that could have changed our lives for the better if they hadn't been crushed by their creators' fears.

I am fairly certain we will never find a way to remove fear from the start-up equation. However, we *can* learn better ways to understand fear and to use it to our advantage. The best way to do that is to look to successful entrepreneurs. They had (and continue to have) fears just like everyone else. But the difference is that instead of letting their fears get the best of them, successful business owners find ways to take their fears along for the ride and actually use them to propel their business forward.

Fear is Healthy

The good news for entrepreneurs is that fear is a very normal emotion. Our bodies are designed to employ fear to avoid risky or dangerous situations. This goes back to the very primitive limbic brain system that we talked about in Chapter 3. In our early human existence, when a tribe member went out on their own or was separated from the tribe, they were vulnerable to the elements, to larger prey, and to death. It was a good rule of thumb to never get separated from the tribe. And there was safety in sticking within the norms of the group. In today's world, when we present a new business idea, the primitive limbic system interprets it as us stepping out of the comfort and protection of our "tribe" and therefore engages our fear response and our "flight or fight" reflex. Hence the stress reactions we get (sweaty palms, dry mouth, numb fingers, etc.) when we are in fearful situations like speaking in public, presenting a new business idea, or, in my case right now, writing a book.

I take comfort in knowing that no matter who we are, we all face the same fear responses. Take the Navy SEALs for example. The Navy SEALs are one of the US military's most elite special operations forces. They undergo twenty-six weeks of grueling training to weed out the unfit and gain the training they will need for combat. Based on what we see in the movies, most people assume that the SEALs are an enormous, hard-bodied, and fearless bunch of men. But what most people don't realize is that in SEAL training, a person's physical capability is far less important than their mental toughness. The secret to getting through the twenty-six weeks of hellish training is to overcome your fears by being laser-focused and committed to your WHY.

Navy SEALs and "Suck" Levels

A close friend of mine and former SEAL (who for the purposes of this book we'll call Oscar) tells the story of a world-class triathlete that went through training in the class before him. This guy was a physical specimen at 6'2". He was an incredible swimmer and runner (think Michael Phelps-like physique). And he made the physical training tasks like pushups, pull-ups and sit-ups look like a breeze. His colleagues say he was the guy you wanted to hate, but you couldn't even do that because he was an all-around nice guy. Upon entering training, everyone bet on him to be the top performer in the class. But, just like anything in life, you can never judge a book by its cover. Or in this case, you shouldn't judge a SEAL by his body type.

Training kicks off with anywhere from 100-200 candidates. In addition to physical tasks, SEAL cadre start to ratchet up tasks that test mental toughness. They call this, "raising the suck level" and they use a scale of 1-10 (with 10 being death).

The whole point of raising the suck level is to test the candidates' mental commitment to the program and their ability to overcome their fears. On one day, the cadre may raise the suck level to 3 or 4 and see who drops out. Then they will drop it back down for a short period. Then the next day they will raise it to a 5 or 6 and again they see who drops out. Within 5-8 weeks they will lose over 50% of the candidates. In the end, they are looking for people whose commitment level goes all the way to 10 without fail. In other words, they are looking for the small, yet committed group of people that would choose death over failure. And often times it's not the most physically fit person who has the most commitment to their WHY.

In the case of the triathlete, he never made it past the second week of training. In a 45-minute cold water endurance session, he couldn't handle the exposure to the cold. His low body fat probably had something to do with it. Meanwhile, his well-insulated neighbor who lacked the same chiseled physique, was one of the few guys who made his way to final group of twenty-two successful graduates. The triathlete wasn't able to put his WHY above his fear of not being able to survive the cold water.

His story can teach us all something. The SEALs are an intensely committed group that would do anything for each other regardless of the situation or circumstances. The only reason they can confront their fears is due to their intense and collective WHY to protect one another and to protect our country. When I asked my friend what his biggest fear was as a SEAL, his voice lowered a bit and he quietly said, "My biggest fear was to fail by dying and letting someone else down."

The bottom line with fear is that it will never go away. We cannot wish it away nor will it out of the normal personal development cycle of an entrepreneur. Some people may be more or less fearful than others, but we will never truly eradiate fear. Nor should we want to.

Fear Helps Feed Your Intuition

Fear is a very important element when you are deciphering whether or not a venture is worth pursuing. Your fear can be a compass for your soul. When you experience fear, the physical reaction tells you the degree of importance your subconscious assigns to the task or idea.

For example, I get the opportunity to speak at a large convention for thousands of women entrepreneurs every year. And no matter how many years I do it, it still scares the living heck out of me. Last year, I spoke to a room of approximately two thousand women. Now, mind you, public speaking is NOT my favorite thing in the world to do even though I'm very capable at it. Having to spend countless hours writing, developing, and perfecting a speech can be exhausting and draining for me. However, my love for developing women who are hungry to learn more about how to be better business owners is something I could do every hour for the rest of my life. So, in the case of the annual convention, I have to acknowledge my fear and understand what it's telling me. In this case, it's telling me that in order to fulfill my WHY of helping women empower themselves through business, the speaking engagement is something I need to tackle. And when I consider the alternative of turning down the opportunity, my disappointment would be larger than my fear.

What I end up reminding myself of each year is that the fear, although scary, is the fuel that creates adrenaline which then enables my mind and body to act together to produce some of my best moments. Knowing that, now I appreciate fear for what it is rather than wishing away its absence. I'm comforted by author Stephen Pressfield who says in his book *The War of Art*, "The more scared we are of a work or a calling the more sure we can be that we have to do it." And your WHY must always be bigger than your biggest fears to ensure you will push through and endure.

And thus, I find the WHY to agree to speak at the convention year after year.

The Five Biggest Fears

The list of fears we have in business could go on and on, but in the thousands of conversations I've had over the years with prospective business owners, here are the five most common:

- Fear of failure

- Fear of not being good enough

- Fear of not having enough time

- Fear of not enough money

- Fear of what people will think

So, let's look into why we have these fears and what we can do to prevent them from slowing our progress on our business journey.

1. Failure

Of course, every entrepreneur's biggest fear is failure. In fact, I would actually argue that budding entrepreneurs from the military community have an even bigger fear response to the idea of failure than the average person. Here is why....

Zero Tolerance Mindset Doesn't Work

When I initially set out to build a team of leaders in my business, my first reaction was to recruit as many of my smart and talented military officer friends as possible. I knew each of them had great work ethic, their moral compass was intact, and they had the same spirit of service to give back to the community just like I did. Luckily, several of them caught my vision, and joined me right at the beginning of my venture. Yet, after the first couple years of assessing their performance, I was sorely disappointed. Their sales performance wasn't nearly as impressive as other leaders who started at the same time. It took me a while to pinpoint the exact problem. But I eventually figured it out. What I hadn't accounted for was the fact that after decades of military service, these officers had been conditioned to "color between the lines" and had an incapacitating fear of stepping outside their comfort zones. In a nut shell, they were terrified of failure.

When you work in a life and death kind of business like the military, there isn't a whole lot of room for error. Thus, many policies end up having a "zero tolerance" type of tone. As necessary as those types of no-mistakes policies are to military operations, they are not helpful in the start-up environment. Any successful entrepreneur will tell you that if you expect perfection in everything you do, you will end up paralyzed and afraid to move off the starting line. This is exactly what happened to the military leaders in my organization.

Now that I know how to recognize this trait, it's easy to spot and coach people through it. To fight the inbred military ways, I stress the idea of valuing progress over perfection.

Progress Over Perfection

"Progress over perfection. Progress over perfection. Progress over perfection."

Knowing I have a history of suffering from perfectionism, this mantra is something I say to myself almost every day in business. And I find that women are usually the biggest offenders of allowing perfection to derail their vision. So, we have to continually remind one another that progress will always be more important than perfection. This reminds me of a quote from my days in basic training from the great General George S. Patton:

"A good plan (violently executed) now is better than a perfect plan next week."

Think of how many times, we as women are especially guilty of allowing *perfection* to paralyze us from achieving our goals? There are so many examples. It could be that you avoided a phone call because you were scared of not saying the "right" thing? Maybe you had a business idea, but squashed it because you told yourself that it would never work? Or maybe you *did* try to achieve something bold, but it didn't go as planned, and that one failed attempt stole your desire to give it another try. The first step in changing these perfectionist habits is to recognize them. Then, start looking for inspiring examples of those around you who are successfully focused on progress, not perfection.

My daughter is an avid soccer player. I love watching her and her nine-year old teammates play travel soccer almost every weekend. Sitting on the sidelines I am fascinated to see her team's relentless pursuit to improve. No matter how many times they miss a goal, lose control, go out of bounds, or get a slight correction by their coach, they continue playing with smiles on their faces, never failing to give 100% effort all game long. And their energy is absolutely inspirational.

Reward Effort, Not Achievement

I attribute a lot of their brave demeanor to my daughter's coach. I have always admired his style, which is to reward good effort and hard work rather than to shame any mistakes. On paper, it may sound like a softer approach than you would expect at a competitive level of play, but in actuality he is one of the most intense coaches in the league. And with this effective method, he coaches some of the most elite teams in Northern Virginia. His secret is that he builds extreme rapport with the girls and teaches them to strive for self-improvement more than winning. In turn, they feel like rockstars and want to work their very hardest.

Carol Dweck, a leading researcher in the field of motivation and performance, would point out that what my daughter's coach is doing is fostering success by teaching a growth mindset. Dweck's research demonstrates that focusing on the process, the effort, the improvement, the perseverance, and NOT the result or achievement, can pay huge dividends. In fact, by doing this, we can actually train ourselves to overcome fears, be more resilient, and in turn be more successful in business and in life.

What if we built an environment where we all felt like rockstars? In both Dweck's research and watching my daughter's coach, there is a lesson of which all of us need reminding: No matter how old you are, keep your focus on progress, not perfection.

2. Being Good Enough

I recently attended a retreat with other successful businesswomen colleagues where the need for this lesson was reinforced. The retreat was an invitation-only event for those who had achieved new titles and promotions, so I was surrounded by an impressive group of proven leaders.

Our first agenda item during training was to connect with each person's motivation for starting their business: their WHY. As we went around the room and each woman spoke, there were revelations about childhood, marriage, wanting to regain an identity, achieve a sense of security, etc. It was a powerful session and the emotional connection through this exercise was absolutely unbelievable.

But the one thing that was surprisingly noticeable in many stories, was an overall feeling of veiled pessimism from each woman that reflected subtle disbelief she had what it took to achieve her big goals. It wasn't that anyone lacked belief in the type of business they had started, the product they represented, or the system they used. Unfortunately, it was that they still had a shadow of doubt in THEMSELVES. I found this realization completely ironic, because by anyone else's measure these women had already proven themselves successful in title and income level. So why are we as women so hard on ourselves?

Encourage Bravery

The reason for each person's ounce of self-doubt varied that day, but according to Reshna Saujani, founder of *Girls Who Code*, TED Speaker on "Teach Girls Bravery, Not Perfection," the overall problem stems from the way we raise our girls. Think about it. As kids, boys are encouraged to participate in daredevil acts like jumping off the highest playground equipment, playing with weapons, and being bold and aggressive at sports. Yet, as girls we hear things like "act like a lady," "be nice," or "don't be too bossy."

This societal disparity between how we raise our boys and girls creates women who will strive, but only to the degree in which they can achieve perfection. If she falls short or attracts any criticism, she starts second guessing her abilities. It's a perfection or bust attitude.

Saujani tells the following story: When guys are struggling with a coding assignment, they'll say, "Professor, there's something wrong with my code;" the teacher will review the code and offer suggestions. However, when a girl calls for help, the teacher will often find the student staring at a blank screen. If the professor didn't know better, we'd assume that the student spent the entire class staring at the screen. But by pressing undo a few times, we see that the student wrote code and then deleted it. She tried, she came close, but she didn't get it exactly right. Instead of showing progress, she'd rather show nothing at all.

Over a lifetime, this breeds the exact feeling I was surrounded by at the retreat. Unlike men who interpret failure as an opportunity to ask, "What went wrong?" we as women, blame ourselves for an imperfect outcome, and ask, "What is wrong *with me?*"

I'm not here to say that I'm not guilty. In fact, I may very well be one of the worst offenders. I was a straight-A student, my friends will tell you that I am obsessed with keeping our house picked up and "presentable," and I probably will have revised this chapter at least five times before you see it. Where I really notice my insecurity come into play is when I return to the male-dominated military world.

I only don my camo uniform for my Air Force Reserve duty in the Pentagon twice a year, but each session brings out an irrational questioning of my abilities. In my business life, I confidently coach and lead a team of over eight thousand women. But the second I walk through the Pentagon doors, it can easily seem like none of that success matters and it's easy to question what I have to offer. Will I pull my weight? Since I am here so infrequently will they look down on my work? Do I have anything to offer? And once we start the self-doubting it can spiral out of control. Does my hair look ok? Should I have worn a different color of nail polish? Does my butt look big? Does my boss think I'm smart? And all this questioning feeds the internal monster that is wondering, "Am I good enough?"

See how this quest for perfection works? Thankfully, I have had to talk myself through this scenario for almost seventeen years and I've gotten better at standing my mental ground, but it's never an easy battle.

Create the Right Environment

All that said, I think it's important to create an environment where we value effort, progress, and even our failures. An environment where every girl and woman believes:

Her ideas will always be as good as anyone else's.

She can try and fail, because failure is a natural stepping stone to success.

Her self-belief can't be stolen by a person's words, by any tough situation, or by society's norms.

Progress is always worth more than perfection.

So, for the sake of the younger generation in life and in business, I challenge you to think about the way you see the world. Is it perfection or bust? Or are there small changes you can make to help encourage your girls to make bold, carefree attempts at going outside their comfort zone and tackling big things...regardless of the outcome?

As Saujani so eloquently stated, "when we teach girls to be imperfect, and we help them leverage it, we will build a movement of young women who are brave and who will build a better world for themselves and for each and every one of us."

3.   Not Enough Time

We are *all* busy. Anymore, what "busy" used to look like twenty years ago is like child's play now. Today, if you don't work full time, shuttle kids around for hours at night and volunteer for church, school and neighborhood activities, you're probably getting looked at as the lazy one. Our world has become a rat-race of *way* too many competing requests for our time.

Milpreneur Sara Wall recommends understanding the phases of your business and giving yourself a little grace in the times of surge. "It's all about prioritization. For example, when you are in a maintenance or steady phase, feel free to be the super-hero and tackle your to-do lists, your someday, and your bucket lists, all while engaging in all of your regular activities. However, when in a surge, allow yourself to reprioritize some of your to-do list. Maybe the laundry can wait another day, you can eat a premade meal…outsource what makes sense, or simply ask your loved ones for a little help (and grace)! Relish in this opportunity to invest in yourself."

Time was my own personal hang-up when I was transitioning from my home staging business to my social commerce venture. I had two small kids, a husband who was never home, a business that had me driving all over the county to get decorating jobs done, and zero spare hours left over. I didn't know how in the world I would add one more thing to my plate.

But that is the beautiful thing about your WHY. When you see an opportunity that fits into the bigger master plan, you'll find magical ways to make more time appear on a schedule where it looks like there isn't room for any.

And that's exactly what I did. For a period of four super-human months, I was running both my decorating company and starting up my social commerce business. I ran one business by day and the other in the wee hours of the night after I had fed the kids dinner and put them in bed. To this day, I'm not exactly sure how I did it all logistically. All I know is that I was inspired by the extreme excitement of my WHY to empower more military spouses with the idea that the best portable job they would ever find would be the one they could make themselves as a business owner. In harnessing the power of my WHY, I was able to find time that I didn't think was there.

Once I made it up in my mind I was doing it, the rest of the details just fell into place. Of course, now I couldn't imagine my life any other way and I'm so thankful that my friend encouraged me to start. My only regret is that I didn't jump into entrepreneurism sooner.

I recount this story time and time again when I hear a woman who is contemplating business ownership say, "But I'm just *so* busy!" My response is always, "I know. I was too! We are all busy. But is *your* 'busy' feeding your soul? If not, then you should really consider some tradeoffs. I did, and even though I'm still busy now, my soul is being fed and it magnifies my energy for everything else!"

4. Money

Meet Lauren Myers. Her biggest fear in starting a business was whether or not she could justify investing money she didn't have to pursue the opportunity to save her family from financial demise.

Lauren is a fellow United States Air Force Academy graduate and former pilot. She married a member of the elite Special Operations Forces. At twenty-six, she and her hubby could have been models for military Ken and Barbie dolls; both are tall, svelte and beautiful people. She was flying combat cargo missions into Iraq and Afghanistan and he was tracking bad guys. They were truly poster children for the US military.

But fast forward a few years and their life changed drastically. They started their family and things took a turn for the worst. Lauren's older daughter was diagnosed with autism while they were stationed in Germany and far away from family. With that news, her husband, with battle wounds both seen and unseen, left the military in order to be able to be home more often and help provide all the care their daughter would need. With his decision to leave the military, the family relocated back to the US. Sadly, within just a couple of months, Lauren's husband was diagnosed with a severe autoimmune disease that most likely stemmed from his years in combat. The disease would leave him as a shell of his former self, both physically and emotionally. He needed surgery to remove his ailing thyroid and with Lauren's care, he literally fought for his life.

To say this was a stressful time is a giant understatement. Lauren was left jobless. She was the caretaker of her sick husband, searching to find the right resources for her autistic daughter, and raising their newborn baby.

And on top of it all, Lauren was desperately looking for a way to earn an income. They needed money badly to pay for rising medical bills and to pay for their home in the pricey DC area. Additionally, Lauren herself needed an outlet besides being a caregiver. Given her hard-charging and progress-driven personality, the immobility of being a caretaker was making her stir crazy.

Lauren was searching for any and all options, when USAFA classmate and Air Force Reservist colleague, Melissa Parent, introduced her to the power of direct selling, or social commerce. Lauren was very skeptical given that direct selling companies are very popular amongst military spouses due to their portable nature. Yet few see many fruits from their labor. Fortunately, what Lauren saw in Melissa's business with a social commerce platform was a refreshing change to the old "party plan."

Melissa was genuine. She was real. And she could work from home around her kids. She didn't have rooms full of product or host high-pressure parties. She could leverage her social media accounts to share her product. And, she didn't need to be pushy with friends and family. What finally tipped the scales for Lauren was when she saw a post on Facebook where Mel was giving half of her paycheck to support a young boy who had a near-drowning accident. Lauren thought to herself, "If they are that generous with people outside of the team, then I can only imagine how supportive they are *within* the team."

The only problem was that Lauren's family was already financially strapped. Their credit cards were nearly maxed out and bills were looming. Yet Lauren knew that it was a good opportunity to achieve her goals and she didn't want to have any regrets. "I felt like I was in the right place at the right time with the right company and I didn't want to kick myself for not trying, even though it was so far outside my comfort zone."

So, she went for it. The day she put the initial business investment on the small remaining room on her credit card, she said that "she nearly threw up." The fear of using the last of their available financial credit was utterly nerve-wracking and extremely scary, but she did it anyway. As tough as it was, she held tight to her belief that it could also be the answer to her prayers and just the thing she was looking for.

Thankfully, and like fear so often does, Lauren's fear was pointing her exactly in the right direction. Lauren's decision to start her business as an independent consultant was the best thing she could do for herself and for her family. Immediately upon starting and despite the stress in the rest of her life, Lauren says "my business became the joy for me." She was quickly able to assemble a team of leaders and after four years in the business, she rose to the top tier of her company's recognition titles. At the level she achieved, Lauren gets invited to participate in focused committees her company hand-picks from a field of hundreds of thousands.

On the financial front, with the success of Lauren's business the family is now in a completely different financial situation. She fully supports her family as the sole breadwinner with a healthy income that far outperforms what she would be making if she had remained a military pilot. The family has successfully paid off all their credit card debt and both Lauren and her husband are homeschooling their girls in a newly purchased home back in their home-state of sunny California.

Lauren says that the best part for her is that, "I get to be in control. I get to live where I want to live. I can be with my husband and kids every day. I can have the Stay-At-Home-Mom life, but I can have the professional fulfillment and paycheck of a working mom. I can homeschool my girls, be at every function I need to be, every doctor's appointment, and every other little milestone...but I can still grow a healthy and thriving business at the same time and I get to help others to do the same."

Lauren's story is living proof that sometimes your fear can be your best compass. What's the worst that can happen, right? It doesn't work out, and you go back to your current plan.

Risky Business

Lauren's brush with her husband's combat-related illness is a reminder that life throws curveballs. Illness, bankruptcy, and tragedy can literally happen at any moment to any of us, military or not. While we can't always plan for the unexpected, you can (and should) continue to invest in yourself and your future. Whether that means practicing habits that build resilient lives, building support networks in good times (so they'll be there in the bad times), or even starting a business that can provide financial security in the times of uncertainty, come up with your plan now.

As military spouses, there is no better time to try your hand at business than while your spouse is still on active duty and while you have the advantage of a reliable income, medical, and dental benefits. Unfortunately, the statistics show veteran business owners are on the decline.17 Yet there are so many reasons why it makes sense given that the life of a military member puts them in situations that can literally change the course of a life in a matter of a seconds.

Marine spouse and founder of Blue Star Families, Kathy Roth-Douquet, is passionate about the importance of spouses building up the skills required to earn an income. "Spouses' dedication to their member's military unit should *not* trump their desire to work," she says. Given the uncertain nature of the military profession, she encourages spouses to make sure they are capable of some kind of work. Not only can this help to bridge uncertain times and unforeseen circumstances, the sense of self-worth and independence it builds is invaluable. Additionally, building towards a career or business allows for a smoother transition to civilian life for the military member.

5.   What People Think

"There is only one way to avoid criticism: do nothing, say nothing, and be nothing."

— Aristotle

After finishing a distinguished career of over twenty-three years in the Air Force, Col. (ret.) Shirlene Ostrov, went from being the commander at the top of the military food chain to being the newest business rookie in DC. Her insecurity about what people would think of her didn't actually happen as she transitioned out of the military, like it does for a lot of people. Her internal struggle happened later.

Shirlene is a self-proclaimed multitasker who likes to have "a lot of irons in the fire." As a logistics officer for her entire military career, it was a logical choice for her to continue working in the industry and to help stand up the company she now runs as President and CEO, Ares Mobility Solutions. In the company, which now employs up to seven workers and fulfills giant logistics defense contracts, Shirlene remains in her comfort zone. She just chooses to wear a different-looking set of attire.

After getting her bearings in the world of defense contracting, Shirlene began spreading her wings to other endeavors to fill the slivers of her time. As a servant leader, she was looking for some other creative ways to give back to her Hawaiian roots while spending part of her month away from her native home on the islands. When she saw that a Hawaiian Cultural School in DC was in need of a principal, she immediately applied.

The school's response to her application was shocking. They informed her that it would be impossible for her to fill the position because they thought she was "too busy." Between running her business and commuting back and forth from DC to Hawaii each month, they determined she didn't have time to juggle it all *and* run the cultural school.

The news devastated Shirlene at first. And, she reacted like most of us do. She ran through a viscous downward spiral of self-doubting thoughts. "Do they think I'm a terrible mother? *Am* I a terrible mother? Has my family been sacrificing all these years for not? What are other people thinking of me?, etc., etc. But, thankfully, she was wise enough not to let the questioning continue for long.

Shirlene *knew* to her core that there was a need for Hawaiian cultural education in the DC area. The fact that people had questioned her ability to focus actually strengthened her resolve to make it happen. It was her passion. It was the fire inside her. In an ironic test of her belief in herself, she had landed squarely on her WHY. So, she did what any passionate business owner does when they discover the power in their WHY. She went ahead and *did it*...beyond all odds!

Shirlene decided to start *her own* cultural school, which in just a few years of operations has already "dwarfed" the original school to which she had applied. She reports that the school is thriving with happy students, well-paid staff, and the knowledge that they have fulfilled the need for a "halau" (school) in the DC area. Shirlene now realizes that people's doubt in her was completely unfounded and the fear she felt early on led her to do it anyway! After successfully founding the cultural school, Shirlene went on to run in a Congressional race for one of Hawaii's seats in the House of Representatives. Although she didn't win, she set the stage for future endeavors and proved to herself that no matter what people think of her, she is going to passionately follow her WHY in as many ways as possible to bring her strong servant leadership to the people who need it.

Eat the Sandwich

The bottom line is this: With any new venture, there will be fears. There will be people questioning you. And it won't be easy. As Elizabeth Gilbert says in her book *Big Magic*, when you're working towards your passionate WHY, you'll have to endure a lot of "shit sandwiches" that can come in all sorts of forms. And sometimes those shit sandwiches will come in the form of your fears. Just know that they are a normal part of the process. Acknowledge the fears, and as Gilbert encourages, "invite them along for the ride. Just don't allow them to steer the car or take control of the radio dials."

Even as I write this book I find myself thinking ahead to its publication, and I can feel fear rearing its ugly head. But, I have to remember that I'm no different than top-notch triathlete

Navy SEALs, CEOs of companies and nonprofits, or top-producing consultants.

We *all* deal with fear.

We all get scared.

We all hear the negative voices in our head that puts into question our time, money, ability to succeed, what people will think, or our ability to be "good enough."

But it's worth it. Do it anyway. Take a big 'ol bite of the shit sandwich, follow the pull of your WHY, and run after your dreams. Hold on for dear life, embrace the fear, and know that if you are feeling the scary butterflies in your stomach, then you are probably headed in the right direction.

Step on the gas and get ready for the ride of a lifetime!!

Chapter 6

When You Hit the Wall

"Courage doesn't always roar. Sometimes courage is the little voice at the end of the day that says, 'I'll try again tomorrow.'"

— Mary Anne Radmacher (author of Lean Forward Into Your Life)

I have loved the challenge of long-distance running since I entered as a cadet at the Air Force Academy in the summer of 1996 and took respite in the beautiful trails Colorado provided. Throughout my twenty years of running, I have waxed and waned in my intensity, but in my prime I was regularly running 5Ks, 10Ks, and half-marathons and eventually, I completed my one and only marathon.

At the time of the marathon, I was in the best shape of my life and I was eager to run in honor of my friend and roommate who was celebrating her 5-year anniversary in remission from her battle with Non-Hodgkin's Lymphoma.

At the outset of the race, I remember feeling like a rock star. I had adequately trained and the first thirteen miles went by with no issues at all. By the second half, I was slowing down from my normal 7:30-8:00 minute pace, but I still felt great. Until I got to mile twenty-one....

Then, SMACK!

It happened.

I hit the wall.

All of sudden, my legs felt like they were filled with lead. I felt like I couldn't make it another five miles and I so desperately wanted to quit. I remember tears involuntarily beginning to stream. I remember I cried for one whole straight mile.

After what seemed like the longest and most painful two miles of my life, it passed. At the end of my emotional outburst, I was able to talk myself down and remind myself that I had trained beyond this point many times and that this wave of fear and exhaustion would most certainly pass. It did and I was so glad I hadn't given in to my doubts.

Just like a new military member in boot camp, or any athlete, every entrepreneur "hits the wall" at some point in their journey. And you will continue to run into your proverbial "wall" many times after that. But what I've found is that how you react to your difficulty at the wall makes all the difference in the long-term success of your business. In this chapter, you will learn that you can teach yourself the kind of mindset needed to push through any and every wall or roadblock that gets in your way. And if you do it right, you can begin to look forward to these challenges, knowing you have the tools to grow through the hardship and to improve on the other end.

Reframe Your Failures

In interviewing the successful military entrepreneurs I've highlighted in this book, I asked each one if they could tell me what their biggest failures were and what they learned from them. I was planning to write this entire chapter on their lessons learned. Surprisingly though, what I got back was not what I was expecting. Rather than a laundry list of proud failures, what I discovered was that most of my successful interviewees had a hard time recollecting ANY failures at all.

I'm certain that their difficulty in recollecting wasn't due to the fact that they hadn't failed in life. Since I asked each person pointedly about their most defining failures, I was shocked to discover that their responses included very few negative words. Instead, my interviewees referred to their failed experiences as "ideas that didn't go as well as we had hoped," "a good try that I was able to learn a lot from," "a chance not taken," or "an opportunity to try again."

Funny enough, once I began to self-analyze, I realized that I would have a hard time pinpointing any major failures in my own business journey too. Even though I certainly have my own laundry list of failures. Instead, if I were asked about times when I had failed, I would have responded with experiences where I "could have done better," or where in hindsight, "I could have made better choices."

What I glean from this is that successful entrepreneurs, and successful people for that matter, reframe failure into a different category in their mind. Because they don't get paralyzed by failed experiences, successful people instead use them to fuel their fire. We see this through history over and over again.

Let's take a look at a few notable examples:

- Professional basketball legend Michael Jordan was cut from the high school basketball team his junior year, only to go on to become one of the most recognized basketball players of all time as a six-time NBA champion.

- Dr. Seuss had his first book rejected by twenty-seven publishers before he went on to become a household name in children's books.

- Oprah Winfrey was demoted as a news anchor because she "wasn't fit for television." She went on to become one of the wealthiest women in American history with her own network and daytime hit show.

- Walt Disney was fired from the newspaper he worked for and was cited as having "no imagination." Luckily, he didn't let that label stop him from building the Walt Disney theme parks and entertainment brand.

- Steve Jobs was the founder of Apple before his own company leadership had him ousted from the company. He later returned to build Apple into the cutting-edge market disrupter we know it as today.

- And finally, our respected sixteenth president, Abe Lincoln (who we all revere as the man responsible for ending the Civil War) was defeated in a whopping eight elections before getting elected president!

Imagine how history would change if they had let failure get in their way?

The theme that runs throughout all of these "famous failures" is the fact that none of these enterprising individuals let the walls they ran into get the better of them. In fact, in all of their cases, just like the military entrepreneurs I interviewed, they used these setbacks to fuel the fire that was burning deep inside of them and achieve their dreams.

What's Your Natural Mindset?

Carol Dweck, one of the world's leading researchers on motivation has spent three decades researching the topic of mindsets. Dweck shows people that the mindset a person adopts for himself or herself can heavily influence the way they approach life. She uses her research to help people realize the impact their mindset has on their achievement in business, in education and in relationships. She also believes that everyone is not stuck with the kind of mindset they naturally adopt. Our mindset is moldable and can be reprogrammed with enough focus and desire.

In Dweck's book, *Mindset: The New Psychology of Success*, she explains that people all fit into one of two mindset categories with regard to their belief in their talents and abilities. You either possess a "fixed mindset" or a "growth mindset."

Fixed Mindset

As Dweck defines it, "A fixed mindset assumes that our character, intelligence, and creative ability are static givens which we can't change in any meaningful way and success is the affirmation of that inherent intelligence."

In a fixed mindset, a person believes that their abilities are innate and cannot be improved or changed. A fixed mindset believes that a person only has a certain amount of a trait, like intelligence or talent, and that is all they will ever have.

I tend to think of the fixed mindset as the "glass-half-empty" type of people in the world. Typically, they don't want to be convinced that there could possibly be more to a story than meets the eye. They won't entertain trying something new because "that's not the way it's always been done." You know what I'm talking about if you have a person like this in your workplace or in your household.

With their fixed mindset, they believe that the world is very black and white. There is a right and a wrong answer to most questions. People are either smart or they are dumb. An entrepreneur is either good at business or they are not.

They have a hard time seeing the shades of grey in between their very binary labels for things.

Growth Mindset

Conversely, the opposite of a fixed mindset is what Dweck calls a growth mindset.

She says, "A growth mindset thrives on challenge and sees failure not as evidence of unintelligence but as a heartening springboard for growth and for stretching our existing abilities. Out of these two mindsets, which we manifest from a very early age, springs a great deal of our behavior, our relationship with success and failure in both professional and personal contexts, and ultimately our capacity for happiness."

With a growth mindset, a person truly believes that they can develop their abilities by practice, dedication and help and from mentoring from others. In a growth mindset mind, a person believes it is possible that everyone can improve himself or herself with the right dedication.

People with a growth mindset are the "Pollyanna" people in your life. They see the glass as half full. They find the silver linings in everything and constantly seek to learn from successful situations and from intimidating ones. With a growth mindset, a person feels like anything is possible and they will continue trying until they figure out how to get there.

Have the Tenacity of a Child

The first example of an undeniable growth mindset in my life is my two children. Right now, they are on a mission to convince Mr. Milpreneur and I that we need to get a dog. We lost our beloved family dog a few months ago and they have been researching on the Internet incessantly to find the next one, despite the fact that we've made it clear we won't even consider it until after our summer travels are complete.

But they just keep coming at us from different angles. When they approach me, they know I'm a sap so they take an emotional approach:

"Oh, Mom this husky is great with kids...and he was abandoned by his owners just a few miles away, and needs a good home." (insert sad face).

With my husband, they go the more logical route:

"Dad, come look, this one is the best dog breed possible for minimal shedding and anxiety and I plan to feed and walk him every day so you don't have to."

They just keep plugging away...day after day...week after week. And they are determined to keep working on us until they prevail.

I am grateful that my kids see the value of using a growth mindset on their quest for the dog, because research shows that over time it produces better results.

In one of Dweck's most famous studies, she gave children the choice of redoing an easy jigsaw puzzle that they had completed before or they could try a more difficult puzzle. What she found was that even as young as age four, these kids already had a God-given mindset.

The kids with a fixed mindset chose to redo the puzzles they had completed before, avoiding any chance that they would make a mistake and "get it wrong." On the contrary, the kids with the growth mindset were confused as to why a person would want to redo something they had already mastered. Instead, they chose the harder puzzle. They preferred to challenge themselves to get out of their comfort zone because they naturally believed that they had the capacity to learn and grow. And the threat of doing it "wrong" didn't even cross their minds.

Good thing my kids have a growth mindset and keep trying despite their initial failures. If Carol Dweck were studying *my* children, she'd probably inform me that we'll most likely have a new dog by the end of this book.

In another study, Dweck tested over 700 seventh-graders for their natural mindset and then monitored their results for the next two years. Her research clearly showed that there was a great divide in their achievement. The grades of the students with a fixed mindset steadily declined, while the grades of the students with a growth mindset steadily increased. This proves that there is immense power in the way we think about our circumstances.

Thankfully, Dweck has also proven that even though you may start with a natural mindset, with enough education and encouragement we can be taught to shift towards a growth mindset. We can do this by learning to praise ourselves and our families and co-workers for their efforts, not their outcomes. Just like my daughter's soccer coach, we can focus more on the fact that we put in 100% effort rather than whether we score. No matter what the environment, rather than beating ourselves up for not meeting the sales milestone or for getting the A, we need to praise ourselves for doing the work and learning from our experiences.

Growth Mindset in Your Business

The growth mindset that Dweck researched in children has a lot of application to our businesses, too. Whether you are just starting out in business or you are a veteran of many years, you can see examples of both types of mindsets all around you. Typically, those who succeed will most likely be the ones who either naturally have or have learned to have a growth mindset. They are the entrepreneurs you see who can hit the wall, maybe even multiple times, and keep forging onward towards success.

In my first business venture, my business partner was dead set on the idea that we needed to complete our own bookkeeping because that was the way she had always done it in her previous businesses. Therefore, she believed it was also the "right" answer for our joint business. Since she had more experience that I did, I followed her lead. But unfortunately for both of us, I quickly discovered how terrible I am with deadlines when it comes to spreadsheets and ledgers. I'm more than capable at completing these tasks, but it takes me so much longer than it should because my mind thinks in big concepts and creative ideas, rather than the detail and tedious care required for bookkeeping. Consequentially, I was always late on turning in my ledgers because even the thought of shoring up accounts at the end of the month was dreadful.

In the Air Force, after any important maneuver or exercise, we follow it up with an after-action report called a "hot wash." When I take an after action look back on this situation, I can clearly see Dweck's research at play.

My growth mindset was quick to realize that we should adapt and hire someone to do the bookkeeping because they could easily spend a fraction of the time I was spending. That would save us valuable time we could be out completing jobs and acquiring new customers (and it would save a lot of hours of heartache on my part). But her fixed mindset still saw the cost of hiring a bookkeeper as a loss. And so, we slaved away for a few more years before we made the change. Oddly enough, in my mental "hot wash" I still don't count this situation as a failure, even though the lost opportunity cost was great, because I learned so much from the experience.

Climbing the Mountain is Easier with a Growth Mindset

> *"In any given moment, we have two options: to step forward into growth or to step back into safety."*

— Abraham Maslow (psychologist and creator of Maslow's hierarchy of needs)

One of the clearest examples of a business leader with a growth mindset is history-making explorer, mountaineer, West Point instructor, and bestselling author, Alison Levine. Levine completed the adventure Grand Slam by climbing the highest mountains on all seven continents and skiing to the North and South Poles. She is a highly sought-after speaker who has graced the stage at TED and countless business conferences. I heard Levine speak several years ago, and the lessons she spoke of regarding setbacks and failure have never left my mind.

From the get go, Levine adopted a glass-half-full mentality because she was dealt a hard set of odds from birth. Not only was she born with a congenital heart defect, but she also suffers from Raynaud's disease, which affects the flow of blood to small arteries in the extremities, and causes them to constrict and cut off blood flow. The loss of blood flow can be exacerbated by cold temperatures, making mountain climbing and traveling to polar regions extra tricky.

In her recount of her attempts to summit Mount Everest, Levine eloquently described that in order to acclimatize to the 29,000-foot mountain, you spend several months strengthening your lungs and legs to reach a number of strategically positioned camps (Camps 1, 2, and 3, and High Camp) that span the mountain on the way to the summit. But what most people don't realize is that it isn't as simple as just ascending from one camp to the next.

Sometimes Progress Means Going Backwards

For weeks, teams acclimatize by a series of upward climbs and descents. For example, Levine describes it like this:

"First, you spend a few days at base camp getting used to the altitude. Then you climb to Camp 1 and spend the night. And then you come back down to base camp. Then you climb to Camp 1 again and spend the night. Then you climb to Camp 2 and spend the night. And then the next day, you come back down to base camp. The next round you go all the way to Camp 3 to 24,000 feet. Then you go all the way back down to base camp."

She describes the weeks of up and down as physically tough as you get used to life on the largest mountain in the world. But she described it as a "super frustrating" process psychologically, too. Despite the physical and psychological hurdles, Levine was learning important lessons along the way.

One of the places I've seen this at play in business is watching the range of emotions that happen when a *milpreneur* gets the news of their spouse's impending deployment. The deployments can range from four months to a full year. When they first get the news, it can feel like a major setback to some people. Others can have a major "woe is me" initial response. "Who will help with the kids?" "How will I get it all done?" "How will we be able to do it all without you?" It can feel very overwhelming.

But what I've witnessed is that once a spouse gets her bearings and realizes that she can still progress despite the setback, she becomes unstoppable. *Milpreneur* Holly Schlachter had her biggest organizational growth year during the year-long time frame her husband was gone. Just like in mountain climbing, sometimes your "setbacks" force you to collect the energy necessary to complete the next record climb.

> *"Fear is ok. It's a normal human emotion. Complacency is what will kill you."*
>
> **- Alison Levine**

Levine talks about how fear is so important and necessary when you're dealing with the threat of death at any moment on Mount Everest, where you are traversing crevasses and ascending to elevations that exceed the conditions where humans can survive on their own. Fear is constant and very important. And it's not the thing to be scared of. Complacency is what should scare you.

As a military pilot, my husband would tell you the same thing. Complacency kills. That's why they train, train, and train some more on the same emergency scenarios over and over. If trained properly, the day that emergency happens in real life, a pilot will still feel the fear, but he or she will quickly revert to muscle memory to implement the solid techniques learned in training.

It's the same in business. Fear is a very real and important part of the journey. A business owner should expect and predict that you will fear things around every corner. But as we talked about in Chapter 5, fear is the compass that you need to follow in order to continue to find your way. The fear will lead you to the next thing to pursue. When you get complacent in a fixed mindset and stop striving to learn and grow. That's when you put your business at the most risk.

> *"Storms are always temporary."*
>
> **- Alison Levine**

Obviously, weather is a major factor when you're climbing Mount Everest. If you've seen the movie *Into Thin Air*, you've seen how quickly the weather can change within moments. But Levine reminds us that the storms are always temporary. They can't last forever. And the same is true in our businesses as well.

We will most definitely have to weather days that don't go our way, goals that we don't meet, and roadblocks that slow us down, but none of it can keep us down forever. So, wake up every morning with the belief that you can weather any storm and make it through to see the sunshine on the other end of the blizzard.

> *"Conditions will never be perfect. But you don't have to have complete clarity to put one foot in front of the other."*
>
> **- Alison Levine**

This statement is probably what stuck with me more than anything else I heard Alison Levine say that day. And she's *so* right. No scenario is ever perfect in the business world. There will never be sunshine and roses for an entire journey up your proverbial mountain. But you have the choice to take one day at a time to the best of your ability and put one foot in front of another until you reach what feels like it might be an unreachable milestone. And if you teach yourself to keep progressing forward, just a little every day, before you know it, you'll look up and find yourself at the top. You'll look back and smile knowing that you grew in your wisdom, your perspective, your strength and your resilience with every painstaking step that you were determined to take. And it was so worth it!

Alison Levine is a rare human being who tackled feats that most of us will never be able to accomplish. Although she was never technically a military member, as a professor at West Point, I'm sure the cadets have already accepted her as if she were one of the Long Gray Line herself.

I can see why they chose her to inspire the cadets that will become the Army's next generation of leaders. Her lessons are so incredibly relevant to all of us.

So, remember to enjoy the journey. Teach yourself and those around you to think with a growth mindset. Go into every experience with the desire to learn, stretch, and grow into a better version of yourself and a better leader for your business. When you feel the strain of hardship, remember what Alison Levine says:

"The people that stand on the top of that mountain are no better than the people that turn around just short of the top. The summit isn't important. What *is* important is the journey and the lessons you learn along the way and how you're going to use those lessons to be better and stronger on the next mountain.... There are always more mountains to climb, so go forward and be even better."

Five Steps to Pushing Through When You Hit the Wall

When I coach women in business, a lot of what I am doing is training their brains to migrate away from the traditional fixed-mindset labels we are so trained to care about in society and to embrace the growth-mindset idea that no matter what the outcome of a task or a puzzle, there is always a way to see the silver lining where we can learn and grow from our experiences.

Here are five steps that I use in coaching that may help you break through your walls too:

1. Know That Roadblocks Are Coming

As with anything, knowing is half the battle. Mentally, you will want to set a realistic expectation for yourself regarding what it means to be an entrepreneur. Despite what it may look like on TV, the reality is that it is some of the hardest work you may ever do. Each industry and business model has their own unique challenges that may make things more or less hard. But no matter what, business ownership is challenging. I've heard it said many times before, "if it were easy, everyone would be doing it." And it's true.

Entrepreneurship requires intense commitment. It may involve late nights, at times you may flirt with failure, and you'll need a whole lot of heart and vision without any guarantee of success. But the truth is that the WHY that drives you, and the dream you can achieve on the other end of your hard work are totally worth it.

2. Be Willing to Adapt

When you encounter difficulty and failure, be aware of your natural mindset and be willing to learn and employ more of Carol Dweck's growth mindset to adapt and overcome. Even though you may launch your business with a very specific and well-thought-out business plan, it doesn't mean that you will always follow it to the letter. Things happen. Circumstances change. The conditions will not always be in your favor. So, be nimble and ready to react to whatever business karma sends your way.

3. Let Failure Fuel Your Fire

If there is one thing that I've learned in talking to all the successful *milpreneurs* in this book, it is that they have an insatiable desire to succeed. Every wall they hit is interpreted not as a failure, but rather as an opportunity to fuel their fire to improve and get better. On my toughest days, I use the mantra my good friend and mentor taught me to say:

"I will always be tougher than this business."

Say it and believe it. Then approach every task with that kind of mindset.

4. Look for the Lesson in Everything

When using a growth mindset, you will see the world from a half-glass-full kind of perspective, and it will be easier to see the useful lessons in every situation. Train yourself to learn through every success AND every failure. Practice finding the silver linings and hidden nuggets of wisdom that can help you improve every single day.

5. Embrace the Power of "Yet"

And finally, when you find yourself going down the road of negativity and you have the urge to use unhelpful self-talk like, "I'm not a good public speaker like Alison Levine," go one step further. Try adding the word "yet" to the end of your statement.

"I am not a good public speaker like Alison Levine, yet!"

It's amazing what power there is when you believe you have the ability to learn, grow, and change your situation because of it!

Chapter 7

The Juggle

With any start-up venture, there is a lot to juggle. Between family, day jobs, wellness, and the overall stresses of our busy lives, there are a lot of things competing for our attention. How many times do you feel like there are thirty hours of work to do in just twenty-four hours? I certainly do. There are days when I say to my husband, "It feels like I have three full-time jobs!" Despite what feels like an overwhelming list of tasks, it all gets done eventually. So, how do we do it all? And how do we balance the rest of our lives?

Get Organized

I am one of those people who easily falls prey to the lure of what I call "shiny objects." These days the world is constantly filled with these distracting shiny objects: social media, texts, online shopping, Pinterest, etc. On any given day, if I don't have my ducks in a row, I can easily be derailed by any of these sexy distractors.

To add to the fun, I'm not a detail-oriented person by nature. I love dreaming up new, big ideas, but when it comes to the execution of having to put my ideas into detail-oriented structures on a spreadsheet or in a budget, I fail miserably. Therefore, I've had to teach myself ways to overcome my tendencies and surround myself with the right people and the right systems to achieve success. These epiphanies didn't happen overnight for me. They were discovered through years of trial and error, learning what works and what doesn't work to help me achieve successful production in my business. I hope you can learn from my many trials so that you don't have to make them for yourself.

Organize Yourself

Whether you are working full time and starting your business on the side, staying home full time and adding your business into the nooks and crannies of your day, or working on your business full time, organization is going to be one of the most critical factors to keeping yourself on track and profitable.

1.   Organize Your Day

We all have a natural time of day that is our most productive. For me, it's in the morning. I don't remember always being a morning person, so I suspect that this habit was formed from my early days in military basic training. And it still stands today. My ideal day includes an early-morning morning wakeup and physical exercise, and then my hardest projects are the first things I tackle with a fresh brain.

Apparently, I'm not alone in this discovery. According to the Bureau of Labor Statistics, the typical American is at work for approximately 8.8 hours every day. Yet, in a surprising study of approximately two thousand British office workers by vouchercloud.com, they revealed that employees were only focused on "work-related tasks" for just slightly less than three hours of that time. The rest of the time people were distracted by a variety of things that are listed below.[21]

The Top Ten Unproductive Activities That Distract Us from Work:[22]

1. Checking social media – 47% (44 minutes, spent doing this during working day).

2. Reading news websites – 45% (one hour and five minutes).

3. Discussing out-of-work activities with colleagues – 38% (40 minutes).

4. Making hot drinks – 31% (17 minutes).

5. Smoking breaks – 28% (23 minutes).

6. Texting and instant messaging – 27% (14 minutes).

7. Eating snacks – 25% (eight minutes).

8. Making food in the office – 24% (seven minutes).

9. Making calls to partners and friends – 24% (18 minutes).

10. Searching for new jobs – 19% (26 minutes).

In order to make your work day the most efficient it can be, it is important to have a good game plan. I have always found that

I am *the* most prepared to tackle a day when I know the night before exactly what lies ahead. If I plan out my week and my days on Sunday evening, I feel much more prepared going into even the busiest of weeks. And it usually starts with making a list.

Make Lists

I am a list maniac. Call it an obsession, call it being control crazy, call it what you want, but lists are my jam. My infatuation with them was born when I was a cadet at the Air Force Academy. The Academy is one of the most strict and rigorous college environments you could ever fabricate. Cadets have very little control over their lives. As first year cadets, or "doolies" as we were called, our lives were closely controlled by the institution's strict set of rules. We could not talk to upper-class cadets without getting permission. We couldn't use the telephone during the week. We had to run along perpendicular marble strips in order to navigate the long distance from the dorms to the academic buildings. And we were even limited in the number of chews we were allowed between each bite of food during meals. We were only allowed seven.

Despite being forced to conform to many rules, I found an inner sense of completion by keeping to-do lists. We didn't have smartphones back then, so my lists were always on paper in good old-fashioned notebooks or on Post-it notes. And even if the military rules forced me to cut my hair a certain way, told me how to march to school, and mandated how long and how many chews I could take when eating lunch, I could still feel like a sense of completion and self-satisfaction when I finished my list of tasks.

As a business owner, I have discovered that when I make a list I am 100% more productive in a day than when I don't. And it makes me so happy to get it all done. I absolutely live for the euphoria that comes with crossing something off my list. In fact, I may or may not be guilty of putting a couple of items on the list that I've already completed, just to get the satisfaction of crossing them off (yep, it's weird.) But the bottom line is that lists keep me on track and keep me accustomed to the feeling that comes along with progress and completing tasks on a regular basis. My lists are always time-bound for that day as well, so there is a certain element of urgency to get it all done before the clock runs out. As silly as it may seem, the game of completing your list is one of the best habits to get into as a business owner. It keeps you productive, it keeps you moving, and it keeps you accountable.

Get Moving

The other thing I have to keep myself accountable to is making sure I physically move my body enough in a workday. I have always enjoyed getting outdoors to run with my dog, taking early-morning walks or just generally getting out in the sunshine and drinking in the fresh air. I KNOW I am truly at my best, both in terms of creativity and production, when I am exercising on a regular basis. However, it is very easy to slip into the habit of sitting far too much and moving way too little as you grow and develop a business.

Research shows that exercise produces multiple benefits that can lead to increased productivity while you work. First, getting your heart rate up can increase the endorphins in your brain, which lifts your spirits and put you in a better mood. Second, it strengthens your body and improves your confidence. When your confidence is high, you have better focus, you need less time off and you are more pleasant to be around.

Dress for the Part

Another thing that puts me in the mindset to be productive is to get ready in the morning both physically and mentally as if I am going to the office. I take a shower, do my hair and put on makeup. There is something very powerful about the mind-body connection of performing a habitual routine like showering and getting dressed to go to work every morning. And it primes my mind to be more "on my game" than I would be without following this morning routine.

Business coach, public speaker, and author Tony Robbins is a major proponent of having a strict physical routine to jolt your body into action in the morning as well as prime your mind for positive thoughts and actions.

In Robbins' case, the first thing he does in a day is he jumps in a Jacuzzi to loosen up his muscles. Then he takes a cold plunge into a shockingly cold shower. The reason he does this is because it resets his nervous system and allows his mind to start in a fresh and rejuvenated manner. Mr. Robbins is a firm believer that "the way you move determines the way you feel."

Therefore, he completes the routine with a nine-minute series of thoughts. The first three minutes he thinks about simple things he is grateful for. According to Robbins, "when you are grateful, you cannot be simultaneously angry or fearful." The second three minutes, he allows his body to feel enveloped by the spirit of God. He focuses on these three minutes to heal his body and solve his inner turmoil. And finally, he finishes by envisioning three actions he will take during the upcoming day. Robbins believes that if we prime our mind and body in the morning with rituals, we can determine the course of our day. As he says, "If we don't take control of our environment, our environment can take control of us."

2.   Organize Your Work Space

My good friends know how much I appreciate a clean house and a tidy office. I mean, I really (really) care. I love to live and work in a beautifully arranged space. I have always believed that the way we feel when we look at our physical surroundings has a major impact on our lives. So much so that my entire first business in decorating and home staging was centered around this concept. I wanted people to love their home space so they could feel calm, settled, and happy even if they had just moved in.

I'll never forget my "office" when I first started as an entrepreneur. It was in the middle of the front room in my house, and during the day it was surrounded by kids' bouncy toys, a baby swing, and often cluttered with mail and other things that needed to go out the door. Because it was a dumping ground, it was absolutely impossible to focus there.

Apparently, there was good reason for my inability to work in a messy office space. In case you didn't know, paper clutter is the #1 problem for businesses. According to the National Association of Professional Organizations, paper clutter causes approximately 4.3 hours per week of wasted time searching for papers and the information contained in them. The Small Business Administration confirms that paper is a major problem because small businesses report that they cannot properly service customers, improve sales and grow their profits due to mishandled paperwork.

So, take some time when deciding on your workspace and how you will set it up and organize it. Invest in a great scanner and shredder, and then commit to a process to deal with your papers. Make a little up-front investment in making sure you love the way you feel in the space, and you will have a good process for ensuring paperwork doesn't pile up.

3. Organize Your Schedule

There are so many things competing for our time in our world today. I've found that the best way to combat the feelings of being stressed and overwhelmed, especially when you are growing a business, is to take control of your own schedule.

Set Up a System

The first step is to set yourself up with a good system. Whether you choose a calendar on your phone like iCal or Outlook, a paper planner, or something simple like a regular college-ruled composition notebook, you will need a good process in order to stay on track when things get busy. I tend to think that there is no one magical organizational tool. Instead, just look for tool that jives with the way your brain works. I tend to get easily distracted, so anything with more than one or two easy steps is not going to be a good choice for me. Therefore, to schedule calls and appointments, I have chosen a simple online appointment scheduling system called Calendly to manage busy times on my calendar and allow for appointments. It's easy and doesn't require many steps from me to create appointments.

I recognize that everyone has a different threshold for what they need when it comes to organizing their schedule. Unlike my affinity for the simple, one step scheduler, I have other friends who love to set two reminders and have all the details about as many aspects as possible related to the appointment as possible at their fingertips. Therefore, it may be worth it for some to have a more in-depth scheduling system. The point is that there is no right or wrong solution, but it's important that you find a good organizational system that works with *your* needs and habits.

Once you know what system you are using, then it's time to schedule out your business hours for the week. I cannot stress enough how important it is to set good time management

habits early on in your business. If you don't do this, it's easy
to fall into bad habit patterns that can waste precious time that
can be spent making progress and revenue.

Like most modern business owners, my business relies heavily
on social media marketing. Therefore, I always have Facebook,
Instagram and Twitter open on my phone or computer all
day long. The notifications are a fun way to get feedback that
posts and content are gaining traction when I put them out.
However, ironically, those same positive notifications can also
be a time-sucking distraction when you are trying to get tasks
done that require a lot of concentration.

Eliminate Distractions

Therefore, I recommend lumping similar tasks into calendar
blocks that are uninterrupted by anything else. For instance, I
may choose to do networking calls from 9:00-11:00 a.m. I put
out my list of people to call and then turn off notifications for
all email, social media and incoming calls. Once I am done with
that, I can block off an hour for writing upcoming posts, again
with notifications turned off. Then I may take an hour for lunch
where I turn my notifications back on. Later, I could finish
the day with one hour of posting and commenting on social
media. There is no right or wrong order, but I guarantee that
if you eliminate your distractions, you will find yourself much
more productive.

Reward Yourself Along the Way

I tend to do my best work from the hours of 9:00 a.m. to noon. If I successfully filter out the distractions during my peak productivity hours, I can get a lot of work done. Additionally, when I first started working from home, I found that I needed a mid-day reward to get myself to keep working continuously until lunch. Starbucks was my answer. If I felt like I was losing focus or energy around 11:00 a.m., I reminded myself that I would reward myself with a nice, warm, white chocolate mocha at the conclusion of another hour. I've used this same reward for myself for over ten years now!

I have also been known to delay the gratification of buying an expensive outfit, handbag or shoes until after I've achieved a big milestone in work as well. When I do this, it makes my work like a game. When I finish, I get a reward. It works with big or small achievements. In my case, just the act of browsing or shopping online is a reward, so I will hold myself back from shopping for a pair of coveted shoes until after I've completed a hard day's work. If I am being extra tough with myself, I may mandate that I can't actually buy them until I've reached an even more impressive stretch goal.

Another thing I caution against, when you are working from home, is doing household chores during your work day. If you are truly 100% invested in growing your business, your housework can wait. Instead, treat your work as if you are actually going to an office. Set up clear business hours that you will be devoting to your business and when the official work day ends, truly end it. Then you can switch into "home" mode and begin working on chores like laundry, vacuuming, etc.

Schedule in Breaks and Days Off

Many eager entrepreneurs will fall into the trap of allowing work to bleed into every hour of every day without clearly defining any time off. As much as start-ups often require this kind of commitment, it doesn't always mean that more hours equal more productivity. I am definitely guilty of being a workaholic. I would spend days on my work without stopping and my husband would have to remind me that I needed a break.

Now I know that in order to maintain an aggressive pace, I have to schedule in breaks throughout the day. Studies prove that fifteen-minute breaks in a work day lead to higher productivity. So, schedule in breaks to move your body and get the creative juices flowing. Also, schedule days off every once in a while. Since most business owners can't just take weekends off like workers at other traditional jobs might, it's important to schedule them in at a rate that can help rejuvenate your body and mind!

Outsource What You Can

Time is truly one of your most precious commodities as a small business owner. There are only twenty-four hours in a day and you will need to use them very wisely to get to profitability as fast as you can. As counterintuitive as it may seem, sometimes the best way to get into your productivity groove is to invest money into outsourcing simple tasks that can easily be done by other people. Things like housecleaning, laundry, yard work, and grocery shopping. There are so many other small business owners who do this kind of work and can save you time so you can focus on what you do best; that is, provide a great product or service through your business.

Balance Isn't Possible

As much as we hear the phrase "work/life balance," I'm beginning to realize that it's rarely ever something I've been able to achieve. Most of us who run businesses around families, military obligations, and other responsibilities know that it's not so much a balance as it is a constant juggle. We teeter back and forth between work and life. And rather than try to achieve the elusive "work/life balance," on most days it's more accurate to simply say, "Work IS life."

4. Organize Your Mind

If there is one thing I know to be true, it's that entrepreneurship is not for the faint of heart. The days can be long. Success doesn't happen overnight. And if you're not in the right mindset, the uncertainty can eat you alive. Fortunately, this is where I believe that the military community has a major advantage, because we are already primed to overcome hardship: we have already endured it for years as military families.

However, there are several ways to organize your mind so that you're ready to put your best self forward. Whether you are just starting out with a new business idea or you have been operating for a while, these strategies for how to achieve your peak mental status will help.

Stay Healthy

When you picture scenes from a new start-up business what comes to mind? You probably see the CEO or founders sitting around a kitchen table late at night drinking coffee and eating-less-than-healthy fare. And oftentimes that picture is not that far from the truth. Business ownership involves lots of long hours, stressful decisions, and uncertainty at times. Because of this, it can be easy to let healthy habits go by the wayside. Yet, the fastest way to halt your production is to lose YOU, so it's imperative that you keep these healthy mental reminders close at hand.

Know When to Say No

As you pour your heart and soul into growing and developing your business ideas, you will find that there will not be enough hours in the day to participate in all the activities and tasks that you were a part of before. So, you'll have to perfect the art of saying "no."

Most of us are terrible at turning down invitations and requests to take on responsibilities. Whether it's team parent, school board, church groups, volunteer responsibilities, or a variety of other things, we are constantly being asked to be a participate or lead things that take up precious time. And the reality is that there are only so many hours in a day. In order to give the time and attention that your business requires to get it up and running and profitable, you're probably going to have to say no to the majority of the things you're being asked to do.

To do this gracefully remember that just because you are saying "no" to an extracurricular for the time being, it doesn't make you a bad person and it also doesn't mean that you'll have to say no forever.

And honestly, it's amazing how liberated you can feel by saying no. A few months ago, I was presented with a dilemma that felt particularly tough to turn down. It was immediately after the busy Christmas holidays and I had just agreed to write this book. We set a short four-month timeframe in which I would write, so I began to critically evaluate the other events on my calendar during that timeframe. I was hit with my first chance to practice this skill within a few weeks. I was asked to attend a business trip that I was honored to be chosen for by my company. I had attended the past three years for this same hand-picked meeting. In years past, I felt expected to attend and made arrangements to rearrange everything to make it happen; however, this year, I felt like I would have stressed myself out trying to juggle the responsibilities of writing this book at the same time.

Implement the Twenty-Four-Hour Rule

I heard this piece of advice a few years ago. It's so simple, yet so powerful and so applicable. When you feel pressure to say "yes" to a request for time, give the decision twenty-four hours before you answer back with a response. In this case of my meeting dilemma, I decided to do just that. I thought through it, weighed my options, and realized that the pros of turning down the invitation outweighed the cons. And then I boldly said "no." Not "well, maybe," and not, "I'm going to think about it." I just said "NO." I wouldn't be able to make it. As hard as it was to say, it was the best thing I could have done. The feeling was incredible. It was like a weight was lifted off my shoulders!

Through this experience, I also learned another great lesson. An honest "no" is better than a half-hearted or strung-along yes. It frees up everyone involved to move on to the next task without hanging on to the hope that you'll come around and say yes. I also learned that nobody was expecting me to justify my response with an excuse. All I needed to say was that I wasn't able to come this year, but that I was so thankful for the invitation. There was no need to give any more explanation than that, even though I mentally walked through fifty different ways I could justify my decision. Through this decision to say "no," I learned so many valuable lessons. People deserve an honest answer and more often than not, a clear "no" is one of the most graceful ways you can respond.

It's a Family Affair

As you mentally prepare yourself to take on the challenges of business ownership, remember that it's not just you that's in business. Whether they know it or like it or not, your family is just as much a part of this venture as you are. They will see it, hear it, and feel it every day right alongside you.

As the child of entrepreneurs growing up, I found this to be one of the most valuable life lessons my parents could have ever given me. I learned so many good lessons about hard work, dedication, teamwork and belief just by watching my parents go through the ups and downs of growing their business. And whether they were having their best or worst year, I learned just as many lessons on either side of the success spectrum.

Now that I am doing the same thing with my family, I can see the light bulbs go off in my children's mind when they watch me grow my business. Not only are they seeing and learning business lessons by watching, but more importantly, they are learning the vital lesson that *anyone* has an equal opportunity to create an idea and turn it into a business if they believe in it and put in the effort to see it come to life.

My big-brained eleven-year-old son approaches me often to ask me if I think he can invent something that could save the world from war, or if he could write a story that would become a best-seller and my genuine response is always, "YES! You can do anything you want to do if you believe in it enough to make it happen." And I don't feel like I'm putting false notions in his head when I say it. He's watched from the front row as I've shown him multiple times that it could be done in our own home.

Be Kind to Yourself

Finally, when it comes to keeping a healthy mindset, you have to give yourself some grace. In interviewing many successful military entrepreneurs, I found one common thread that carried throughout each of their stories was one of self-forgiveness. No business or business owner is perfect. You will never be able to be all things to all people or be in all the places you need to be at any given time. But you're going outside your comfort zone to pursue a dream. You're leaving the mundane life everyone else leads to give it a go. And that's worth a lot.

So, forgive yourself. Forgive yourself for the tradeoffs you make in the short term to see long-term return. Forgive yourself that you miss an occasional soccer game or a family gathering.

Maybe you were a great CEO today, but not a great mom. Maybe you were an amazing spouse today, but you were not able to get everything done on your business to-do list. Or maybe your house is a disaster, but you were able to complete your military duties so you can get back to business.

The fun part about business is that there is no right or wrong path. It's a winding journey that can only be decided by you. Each chapter is intended to help you learn and grow and every experience provides context for the next. Enjoy the ride and be kind to yourself along the way.

Chapter 8

Know Your Resources

As a kid who spent my entire childhood in Montana, I was used to a small-town mindset. Most of my classmates didn't venture very far from home after high school graduation. In fact, most didn't attend college. And for those that did, they usually remained at an in-state school within a day's drive from home. It was rare to see anyone venture to the East Coast or down South, and it was only occasionally that there would be a story of someone making their way to the West Coast to live in Seattle or California. Because most people were content to stay local, the need for knowledge about scholarship opportunities in the rest of the country was not highly sought after.

From a young age, I had goals to travel and see the world. I figured the best way to do that was to go as far away to college as I could. So, I wrote to admissions offices at every Ivy League college on the East Coast and began dreaming about which one I would attend. Then I worked my buns off to gain the number one spot in my class, assuming that was my ticket out of my small town. And I did it. I was valedictorian, topping the ranks of a whopping 155 kids in my class in Laurel, MT.

Now, you would think that graduating at the top of my high school class would land me some amazing college scholarships, right? Unfortunately, that wasn't the case. It wasn't because there was a lack of scholarship opportunities at that time. It was merely due to the fact that I grew up in a sheltered small-town environment and I didn't know what I was looking for. It was before the Internet had become a convenient resource, and I wasn't aware of the opportunities that I should have been applying. I simply didn't know where to look.

I felt a similar lack of awareness when I became a military spouse and was looking for resources to help me start a business. When I would ask my fellow military members or spouses for advice on where to find things like start-up loan money or where to go for business training or mentoring, I would get a lot of blank stares.

Since half the battle in starting up is knowing your resources, I wanted to make sure that I added in a comprehensive list of resources for budding military entrepreneurs. There is a wide array of entrepreneurial resources available to veterans and spouses when it comes to education & training, marketing, sources of funding, and helpful blogs. This list narrows in on my *favorite* programs for military spouses. I carefully formed this list after years of using and evaluating *milpreneur* resources; however, I highly encourage you to search for resources because there are so many programs that provide services at free or reduced costs, and they are changing all the time. Here are my top resource recommendations:

1. Syracuse University Institute for Veterans and Military Families (IVMF)

The Institute for Veterans and Military Families (IVMF) based in Syracuse, NY is one of the oldest programs for veterans in our country's history. After WWII, the institute provided the first-of-its-kind program to welcome veterans home from the war and provide them with money, accommodations, and education. They truly paved the way for others by opening their doors to veterans to participate in higher education.

Today, the institute's staff of more than fifty professionals delivers programs in career, vocational, and entrepreneurship education. Their training provides service members, veterans, and their families with critical skills needed to succeed in education, work, and life.

The IVMF programs are very comprehensive and appeal to all sectors of the military community from disabled veterans, to veteran family members, to guard and reserve members, to veterans who want to learn technical programs. There is also one program that directly applies to military spouses called V-WISE; Veteran Women Igniting the Spirit of Entrepreneurship.

In the V-WISE program, they help women veterans and female military spouses find their passion and learn the business-savvy skills necessary to turn an idea or start-up into a viable business. There are three phases in their program that include a fifteen-day online course, a three-day entrepreneurship training event and continued mentorship, training, and support.

Website: www.ivmf.syracuse.edu

2.   Inc. Magazine Military Entrepreneurs

The Inc. Magazine Military Entrepreneurs program is a wonderful resource to gain business education and mentorship. The program began in 2011 and strives to "help veterans, service members and their families start, grow, and run their own businesses through mentoring, education, networking, resources, and information provided through Inc.'s special events and business conferences."

Throughout the year, the program sponsors eligible military candidates at Inc. conferences in the spring and fall with access to special events designed specifically for the military delegation. They also provide a small special group of entrepreneurs access to a Boots on the Ground regional event series in multiple locations around the country.

I attended this program in 2015 in New York City and found the experience to network and learn from experienced entrepreneurs to be invaluable. We spent the day collaborating with and learning from a variety of successful Inc.-contributing entrepreneurs, including Jay Jay French, founder and guitarist for the band Twisted Sister, serial entrepreneur and senior contributing editor Norm Brodsky, and author Lewis Schiff. I highly recommend this program for anyone looking to expand their start-up to the next level.

Website: www.inc.com/military-entrepreneurs

3. The MilSpo Project

One of the things I noticed right away when I began my entrepreneurial journey at the age of twenty-eight, was that most of the groups that were designed to help military spouse entrepreneurs were run by leaders that were considerably older than me and with differing outlooks on the way businesses should look and run. I was looking for mentors that thought and envisioned the future of business the way I did: online, creative, portable, and collaborative. Yet, I felt like a lot of what I saw was still very traditional and a little bit old-fashioned. I craved a fresh perspective, and yet I didn't see very many resources that appealed to the young, creative entrepreneur.

Therefore, it was a breath of fresh air when I saw The MilSpo Project emerge in 2014. They appeal to the younger generation of military spouse, and they have done a spectacular job of putting a renewed, trendy, and savvy vibe on basic building resources.

Founded by Elizabeth Boardman and a network of younger professionals, the Milspo Project is a "global network of US military spouses who believe entrepreneurship is a unique answer to the military spouse unemployment crisis in our country."

The group seeks to embrace, rather than reject, the unpredictability of military life. They aim to set the tone for what it means to be a successful military spouse professional in today's society. And they connect *milpreneurs* through a membership model to create community in "chapters" across the country, where budding entrepreneurs can lean on and learn from one another.

Website: www.milspoproject.org

4. Bunker Labs

Started by a retired Navy officer, Bunker Labs is a national nonprofit that extends across the country in chapter locations from California to Washington, DC. Their aim is to provide education and training, mentoring, networking events, and a robust community to help *milpreneurs* as they start and grow their business ideas.

They offer a fourteen-day program for early-stage entrepreneurs called EPIC (Entrepreneurial Program for Innovation and Collaboration). In this two-week educational course designed to fit around a full-time work schedule, attendees interact in a laboratory environment to test their business ideas. At the same time, they glean valuable knowledge from seasoned mentors with backgrounds in everything from small start-up ventures to Fortune 500 companies.

In addition to providing education resources in their physical locations, Bunker Labs also provides a service called 'Bunker in a Box' for those who cannot travel to one of their chapter locations. Bunker in a Box provides budding *milpreneurs* with worldwide access to online entrepreneurship education, including an array of interviews from thriving military entrepreneurs who have successful launched businesses in a variety of different fields.

Website: www.bunkerlabs.org

5.   Rosie's List

Rosie the Riveter is an iconic image in the military, symbolizing the need for women as an important part of military strength and progression. And it's the perfect icon for what Rosie's List represents. Stephanie Brown is the CEO and founder of Rosie's List. After she spent hours searching Angie's List & Craigslist for a quality contractor to complete work on her home, she found she was not comfortable hiring a complete stranger. As a military brat and wife of a retired Navy Admiral, she found herself wishing she could hire a veteran instead. So, she set out on a mission to create a way for the average American to be able to find and use military family-owned businesses and Rosie's List was born. Since its inception, Rosie's List has expanded to become the Rosie Network and now includes other services to help connect and empower the military community.

As stated on their website, the Rosie Network's mission is "to build stronger military families by developing entrepreneurial programs and support services that empower military spouses, transitioning service members and veterans, increasing the financial stability and self-sufficiency of American families who serve." Rosie's List includes veteran, active duty, or military spouse-owned businesses and users can leverage the Rosie's Network search tool to find exactly what service they are looking for.

Website: http://rosieslist.org/

6.   Blue Star Families, Blue Star Entrepreneurs

When my family moved to the DC metro area, I knew I wanted
to put my entrepreneurial experience to work to help shape
policy for military spouses. I started doing my research to find
where to begin, and repeatedly I was led to Blue Star Families,
because they have a large membership base and they have
become a go-to organization when it comes to lobbying for
military families regarding legislative policy.

The BSF group was born as a grassroots organization. In
April of 2009, a group of military spouses, including founder
Kathy Ross-Douquet, combined forces with the vision of
making an impact in the lives of military families. They saw a
plethora of challenges faced by military families and created
a platform where military family members could join forces
with the general public and their communities to address
those challenges. They also made it their mission to conduct
thorough research on the military population in order to
accurately know how to help them.

Since its inception, Blue Star Families has grown from a few
military spouses around a kitchen table to a community of
hundreds of thousands of members and communities and
chapters around the globe. Membership is absolutely free, and
they provide a plethora of resources, from free books for kids,

to free access to museums across the country, to extensive employment resources.

The BSF resource I find extremely helpful is their annual report based on their annual Military Family Lifestyle Survey. Each year, BSF surveys the military community of military members, veterans and family members to get accurate and timely statistics on everything that affects military recruitment, retention, and readiness. Within the survey, they gather data on many facets of the military lifestyle that are important to know. They survey areas like mental health and wellness, employment, military children, financial readiness, and suicide. With this data, they are able to effectively provide input to policy makers, corporations, and nonprofits regarding the issues military families face. This survey is not only important to the average military family, but it's also important for businesses and policymakers in order to get in the minds of the military community and find the best ways to find solutions that add value.

Website: www.bluestarfamilies.com

7.   National Military Family Association

The National Military Family Association (NMFA) is one of the most well known sources of military support in the country. They have been helping military families for decades. They are one of the go-to sources for Administration officials, members of Congress, and key decision makers when it comes to military families. On top of all that they do for families, NMFA is also a very useful resource for military spouse entrepreneurs. They provide an array of offerings for new entrepreneurs to get their business off the ground, including some very generous scholarships.

Each year, NMFA awards scholarships to eligible military spouses in several different areas. Typically, they provide four different awards. One award is $500 for career funding, another is $1,000 to pursue a degree, a third is $2,500 for mental health professionals who obtain licenses, and finally there is a $1,000 scholarship for spouses who want to build their own businesses. The scholarship can be used for any type of business, and all ID-carrying military spouses are eligible to receive the scholarships.

Website: www.militaryfamily.org

8. MyCAA Military Spouse Career Advancement Accounts

Over ten years ago, when I started my first business, one of the first resources I learned about was the MyCAA program. The Military Spouse Career Advancement Account (MyCAA) program offers up to $4,000 of tuition assistance to eligible military spouses. The scholarship money allows spouses the ability to pursue any sort of licensure, certification, or degree needed to get hired or start businesses that allow for portable careers and occupations. Spouses receive their funds and are able to use them at any academic institution that has been vetted and approved by the MyCAA program.

The only limitation with the MyCAA program is that only spouses of specific ranks are eligible. At the time of publishing, they include spouses of active-duty service members in the pay grades of E-1 to E-5, W-1 to W-2, and O-1 to O-2. Additionally, the military sponsor must be on Title 10 military orders (or on Active Duty Status).

The MyCAA Scholarship pays tuition costs for education and training courses and examinations contributing to an associate's degree. The scholarship also covers the costs for obtaining a license, certificate or certification at an accredited college, university or technical school in the United States or approved testing organization that expands employment or portable career opportunities for military spouses. For some programs, if required, applicable gear, like a laptop, can also be covered with the scholarship funds.

Website: www.aiportal.acc.af.mil/mycaa/

9. Boots to Business Program (SBA)

I have appreciated Small Business Association resources every step of the way on my entrepreneurial journey. When I first started out, I would check out business books from my local SBA site. Later, I used their mentoring program to get coaching on how to scale my business. They have so many great programs for a new entrepreneur to leverage.

Another one of their useful programs is called Boots to Business. It is an entrepreneurship track under Department of Defense's Transition Assistance Program (TAP). Reboot, which is a course offered through Boots to Business, is designed for military and their families who have left the military life and transitioned back to life as civilians. It includes a two-day in-person course offered at sites around the country and an eight-week online course full of instruction on how to research, start, and run your business.

The Boots to Business curriculum helps guide participants through the entire process of evaluating to find the right business model, learning the right foundational knowledge needed to write a business plan, and finding resources to gain funding.

Veterans of all ages, service members (including National Guard and Reserves) and their spouses are eligible for the Boots to Business Program. And all of the classes, both physical and virtual, are free.

Website: www.sbavets.force.com/s/

10. Streetshares

One of the biggest hurdles a new entrepreneur faces when starting a business is the fact that they need investment capital. Even for a small business that may only require a few thousand dollars, that is still money that, unless you have it readily available in your bank account, has to come from somewhere. After the market crash in 2008, lending became even more difficult to obtain, which added one more hurdle on the journey to start a business.

Thankfully, Streetshares emerged to fill the gap. The founders, Mark Rockefeller and Mickey Konson, envisioned a small-business funding community that would "breathe new life into the American dream." Their business model connects business owners who are looking for start-up funding and investors who are looking to gain financial return along with paying it forward to support other American business owners. They see it as a win-win for all involved.

Streetshares also has a foundation that provides a "Veteran Small Business Award" of up to $5,000 to a set of military business owners each month. The program requires applicants to submit an application and a short video about their plan to grow their business with the award money. Then they select five to ten finalists, and they put it out to a public vote. Winners can earn the top award of $5,000, second place for $3,000 or third place for $2,000. Each year, Streetshares dedicates one month to military spouses. During that month, the competition for the award is limited to just spouses.

Website: www.streetshares.com

11. National Military Spouses Network (NMSN)

Networking is an essential skill to progressing in business. Luckily, the military community is a tight-knit group that has a natural knack for networking to help one another. Sue Hoppin, the founder of the National Military Spouses Network, is a networking expert and put her skills to good use by bringing spouses from across the country together to provide professional development and mentoring, and to empower and advance military spouses on their quest for employment and entrepreneurship.

The goal at NMSN is to prove to military spouses that it IS possible to have a career path that is fulfilling and fruitful AND stay committed to a spouse's military career that causes multiple relocations.

Having attended the NMSN conference in DC twice, what I love about their events is that they are able to attract top-notch speakers from the metro area, but the feel of their events is family-like and low key. I have maintained relationships from several other *milpreneurs* that I met at their events, and I have watched them gain steady success over the years.

Another aspect I really enjoy about NMSN is that they are always at the forefront of what's new in the technology space. Whether it is virtual water cooler chats that spouses can participate in from anywhere around the globe, or lessons on social media techniques, or live videos from their conference, they are committed to keeping their community abreast of what is the latest and greatest in the world of technology for small business owners.

Website: www.nationalmilitaryspousenetwork.org

12. Patriot Boot Camp

Although I have never been to a Patriot Boot Camp, some of my very successful *milpreneur* colleagues have and they give it rave reviews. A nonprofit arm of the start-up accelerator Techstars, the Patriot Boot Camp is offered to active-duty military members, veterans, and their spouses. They provide training and education, mentoring, and a community to help grow successful technology entrepreneurs.

The program was born at Techstars as a volunteer effort to fill the void in support military entrepreneurs were encountering as technology entrepreneurs. PBC's core program is an intensive three-day event designed to engage, inspire, and mentor veterans and their spouses, to help them start, innovate, and scale the next generation of technology-focused businesses.

Interested entrepreneurs will enjoy knowing that Patriot Boot Camp is completely free! Each year the camp is held in different locations around the country and it attracts an array of talented business minds.

Website: www.patriotbootcamp.org

13. Marie Forleo B-School

In this day and age, blogs, videos, and memes litter my news feed on a daily basis. But the one that stands out from the crowd and always resonates with me is that of author, coach and blogger Marie Forleo.

Marie is a creative soul who has vast experience with business start-ups from a very young age. She has done it all. From professional dancing, to writing a book, to a weekly video segment called Marie TV, she has experienced both the good and bad sides of entrepreneurship. She shares her experiences in an authentic and humorous way to help entrepreneurs get ahead in their business. Her efforts and experienced culminated in a course she calls "B-School."

B-school is an eight-week, interactive, video-based training program that teaches smart, effective online marketing strategies to business owners who want more sales and more impact from their online presence. The training consists of weekly modules, with accompanying videos and worksheets. Students are also encouraged to collaborate with other students within a series of private Facebook pages. An added advantage is that once you complete the program, you get access to the resources and community for life. There is no fee to retake the course.

Marie Forleo and B-school also give out a generous number of scholarships each year (usually around twenty), based on video submissions. I have watched the program for years and have seen military entrepreneurs win on a consistent basis, so it is definitely worth looking into.

Website: www.marieforleo.com

14. Simon Sinek "Start With Why" Course

Last, but certainly not least, I want to highlight a program developed by Simon Sinek, who inspired Chapter 3 of this book. Sinek is best known for popularizing the concept of *Why* in his first TED Talk in 2009. It is one of the most popular TED Talks of all time, both across the US and globally. Sinek has been known to have an affinity for the military and highlights several military stories in his book, *Leaders Eat Last*.

From his Ted talk, Sinek developed a "Why Discovery Course" which is an interactive course, filled with 7-10 hours of videos where Simon uses step-by-step exercises to help you discover and bring your Why Statement to life. Normally, this course costs $129, but as a salute to those who serve, Sinek offers it to active US military and veterans for a $10 administration fee. All you need is proof of service or a form DD 214.

Website: www.startwithwhy.com

Just Get Started

Your head may be spinning as you read through all of these resources. But hopefully you also feel your heart racing to know that there are a lot of great programs that you can leverage to get your business to the next level!

The thing to remember is that there is never a right or a wrong answer when it comes to getting started. There is no perfection training. No perfect timing. And no perfect outcomes. Remember, we are always looking for progress over perfection. As an entrepreneur, you'll find yourself saying this to yourself all the time....

Just do it.

Don't spend too much time overthinking which resource to pursue, or wondering if one is better than another. Start somewhere, and then you can refine and redirect as needed for the gaps you have in your knowledge as you see them arise. A big part of the learning and development process is meeting other budding entrepreneurs and learning from their successes and failures, so jump in and start somewhere!

Also, don't think you're "trained" after participating in just one program. If there is one thing I've learned through my experiences, it is that the best entrepreneurs *never* stop learning. They continue to learn, grow, and strive to make new leaps forward in the way they think, lead and conduct their business. Forever.

So, learn to love the process. Find your favorite resources and then keep expanding your list and offering your wisdom and mentoring to those behind you even if you've just learned something. Sometimes your lessons learned, no matter how ugly, may be just the thing that tips the scales for another entrepreneur to make a major breakthrough.

Be a Resource for Someone Else

I cannot begin to thank all the generous mentors I've had over my years in business. Some of the relationships were formal ones where I solicited help and others were valuable lessons I learned from unknowing teachers along the way. But I can say with certainty that after I built my basic knowledge of business through traditional methods, *people* were my best resource.

Remember that as you grow, in the world of entrepreneurship, we all rise by lifting one another. It takes a tribe to become your best. And we owe it to one another to help the next generation to become even better than we ever could.

As for me, you can sure bet that after I left Montana, went off to Colorado for college and then moved over the map with the military, I made it my mission to turn around and share my wisdom with others. The good, the bad, *and* the ugly. It's all a part of the beautiful journey and it is all a lesson to someone. I have no doubt that you will have the chance to do the same!

Chapter 9

Leaving Your Legacy

"I alone cannot change the world, but I can cast a stone across the waters to create many ripples."

— Mother Theresa

What legacy were you put on this Earth to fulfill? Have you ever truly sat down and thought about it? What will your life stand for? What will you leave as a lasting impression?

I've always known that I was born to do something meaningful in life.

The seeds of this idea were planted back in my childhood when I watched my selfless mother serve our community in any way she could. From her service in the Peace Corps, to her years of volunteering as a ski aid for kids with disabilities, to her constant presence at our church, she taught my siblings and me the true meaning of selfless devotion.

As I grew up, the fire was stoked when I began my military service at the age of eighteen. In the Air Force, I learned to think outside my selfish teenage sphere. I learned the value of standing for something in life and how my occupation could support my statement to the world. I also learned the value of being part of something bigger than just myself. Perhaps even more significant, I learned how much my military family would sacrifice to support each other and even me.

Then it all came together when I started my entrepreneurial journey. Even though I was driven to achieve, I saw how my sense of fulfillment resulted less from my paycheck than from watching the reaction of those whom I served. Their smiles were the payment! Whether it was decorating a home for a deployed young mother, helping a woman regain her confidence with a skincare solution after a life wrought with acne, or teaching women how to build businesses and prove they are worthy of becoming their own CEO, every one of my businesses has been driven by a sense of service.

Service Has Power

My experiences have shown me that service, or serving others, is an amazing and powerful force. It can inspire people to give of themselves even when they don't feel that they have much to give. It can drive people to work harder and longer than they normally would, because they care about the welfare of another. It can push people to accomplish incredible feats, innovations, and discoveries beyond what they initially intended. And it can even move people to fight and die for their country or a cause greater than self. The military community knows how to serve better than anyone, and it's an incredible business advantage.

Building upon my foundation from the Air Force Academy, I obtained a Master of Education in Human Resource Development from the graduate school at Colorado State University. I was fascinated with and focused a lot of my studies on the topic of leadership. After learning many different approaches to leadership, I became enamored with and studied the teachings of Robert K. Greenleaf, the father of the concept of "servant leadership."

In his book, *Servant Leadership*, published in 1970, Greenleaf explained:

> *"The servant-leader is servant first…. It begins with the natural feeling that one wants to serve, to serve first. Then conscious choice brings one to aspire to lead."*[23]

Compared to other types of leadership, Greenleaf's servant-leadership seemed very organic and it was something anyone could use in a variety of settings. I studied Greenleaf fervently, knowing his ideas would come in handy when I was able to lead my first set of Airmen as an officer.

In Greenleaf's theories, a servant-leader focuses primarily on the growth and well-being of people and the communities to which they belong. While traditional leadership usually centers around the acquisition of power and a need to get "to the top," servant leadership is exactly the opposite. The servant-leader shares power with his or her organization and seeks to meet the needs of others first. A servant-leader also has a deep desire to help their team develop and perform as highly as possible.

Some famous examples of a servant-leaders are General George Washington, Abraham Lincoln, Mother Theresa, and even Jesus. These servant-leaders put their followers' needs first before their own needs or ego, and the results were history making. Servant-leaders empower and excite people to change the world for the better, even though it's hard. Their intense focus on serving, more than anything else, is what gives them such influence as leaders.

You will also see servant-leadership routinely in military organizations and families, although nobody would think to label it as such. To us, it's just the military way of life, the "esprit de corps" we know and love. The terms "service before self" and "selfless service" are actually included in the Air Force and Army core values, respectively. But they don't need to be written down to know they are alive and well in the military community. You see servant-leadership when you see military members going out of their way to volunteer in the community, military spouses helping other spouses whose member is deployed with childcare or household needs, and the tight-knit military community which has an overall sense of trust and family-like connections. In fact, the military word "sergeant" is even derived from the French word for servant.

Social Entrepreneurship

In his book, Greenleaf reminds us that in any venture, "the work exists for the person as much as the person exists for the work." If we apply this to the business world we can phrase it another way: "the business exists as much to provide meaningful work to the person as it exists to provide a product or service to a customer."[24] This idea of serving a larger community through a profit-generating business is referred to as Social Entrepreneurship.

Social entrepreneurship success stories have grown tremendously in the recent past and they are proving that businesses can achieve solutions to the world's problems *and* turn profits. In fact, you are probably exposed to some of the most well-known examples of social entrepreneurship every day. TOMS shoes, Seventh Generation products, Kiva microloans, and even Combat Flip Flops are all changing the way we think about business.

Let's look at Combat Flip Flops and its unique mission to give back while growing a profitable business. Matthew Griffin, *milpreneur* and CEO of Combat Flip Flops, turned his military experience into a business opportunity that promotes the peaceful change he wants to see in the world. During his several deployments as an Army Ranger, Matthew and his buddies realized that they were surrounded by villages of hard-working and creative people. Inspired by this, Combat Flip Flops developed into an international business that makes apparel and accessories, while empowering the people of conflict or post-conflict regions. For example, Combat Flip Flops makes footwear in Bogota, Columbia, which provides jobs and invests in the local community. Their sarongs are handmade by local women in Afghanistan, and every sale educates an Afghan girl in secondary school for an entire week! And their bangles and bracelets are created by artisans in Laos, using bombs that were dropped in the country during the Vietnam War. With each bracelet sale, three square meters of Unexploded Ordinance (UXO) gets cleared.

Isn't this what life and building your own business is all about? Not only paying the bills, but paying it forward to the causes that are important to you?

It's Time for a Change

But a question still remains. With the military community's natural tendency to serve the greater good (social entrepreneurship) and our knack for servant-leadership, why haven't we seen *more* start-ups from *milpreneurs* that solve society's problems and allow for individuals to find meaning through selfless service?

The reason is simply this: we haven't had enough people try! Until now, there have been very few successful *milpreneur* stories out there paving the way for others to follow. Perhaps it's because the military community is filled with rule followers, and the rules are complex or murky. Perhaps it's because we are ready to jump in only after the risk assessment assures success, and there are no guarantees in business. Perhaps it's because the environment isn't conducive, and more social progression is still needed. Or, perhaps it's because enough of the right trailblazers haven't emerged to tip the scales to create a movement. But after seventeen years as both a veteran and a spouse, I have seen very few people, whether military members or spouses, take the plunge into entrepreneurship and truly leverage their built-in talents in the start-up world, and we can do better.

So, it's time.

Time for a change. Time to step into our potential. And time to start a *milpreneur* movement!

So whatever business idea has been rolling around in your head, give it life.

Give it respect.

Write it down.

Dream of how it will help others.

Solidify *why* this idea will drive you.

Share it with others to gain a sense of what you need to tweak to make it come to life.

And then begin *believing* in it!

As long as your idea addresses a solvable problem in the world, know that it's worth pursuing. The key is that you have to believe in both yourself and your idea.

And, unfortunately this is where most people fall short. They give up. The think their experiences aren't good enough. They think their idea is silly and nobody will need it. They listen to the naysayers that second-guess why they would try to go outside the norm. And then they cave and go back to the status quo. Uninspired and afraid of their greatness, they retreat.

But here is the thing. With your contribution, our military community *can* do this. You are well suited, you have the right skills, and you know how to work hard. Don't sell yourself short and think that you don't have what it takes to build a business like every other citizen out there. *You do*!

There will never be the perfect conditions, the perfect day, or the perfect set of odds. Like preparing for having kids, it just never works out the way you imagined. You just have to jump in and give it a go. And here are a few reasons why.

LIVE

Do It for Yourself

Maybe you had big childhood dreams for yourself, but then the commitments of military life took over and you gave up on them? Now is your chance to pursue that dream again and share your special gifts with the rest of the world. Why not? Studies show that entrepreneurs are happier overall than the average person.[25] And now that you know the resources available to help you, this is your moment to create something of your very own.

You have the chance to create your *own* business that no military move or deployment can take from you. You have the chance to create your *own* paycheck and contribute to your family's bottom line. You have the opportunity to make your mark, discover your calling, build a sense of independence and self-reliance, and improve your confidence that is so important to one's total health. And more than anything, you have the chance to design and *live* a life that can go with you long after you or your spouse's military commitment ends.

Maureen Dougherty says it best when she describes how her experience as a *milpreneur* has allowed her to *live*:

"Before I started my blog, I was a supportive military spouse, but I never felt like I left my *own* mark. Now that I've experienced the power of owning my own business, I am confident I'm leaving *my* mark too. I want to do something incredible and awesome and leave people saying, 'Wow, she did something big!'"

There is nothing like the feeling of being able to truly *live* the life you want and make lasting contributions with your time, energy, and money.

GIVE

Do it for Your Family

There are countless lessons a family learns from being a part of the military community. Of course there are the sacrifices, frequent moves, changing schools, inconvenient deployments, and friends left behind. But the benefits still seem to outweigh the hardships. Kids learn invaluable lessons like the importance of things like hard work, loyalty and respect, and they gain a deep pride and sense of belonging within the military community.

One could argue that the same trade-off occurs when you start a business venture. Even though entrepreneurship comes with some long hours and intense commitment, the benefits you can GIVE your family are priceless and go far beyond a paycheck.

My kids have learned so many important lessons. They have seen that anything is possible when you believe in your idea and you put in the effort to see it to fruition. They have seen the joy that comes from setting a goal and then crushing it. They have seen that failures are just a part of the journey, and they aren't something to avoid or be afraid of because they can also be the stepping stone to the next big development. They have seen that work and family are not mutually exclusive. They can be beautifully interwoven. And more than anything, they have seen that a person's destiny doesn't rely on an employer, on the government, or on anyone other than themselves!

Growing my business alongside Mr. Milpreneur's full-time military career has allowed us to get ahead financially and it's provided choices and stability that I didn't think we'd achieve until much later in life. But we didn't start that way (remember the five-dollar-a-day budget?). Thanks to my business, we've been able to send our kids to fantastic schools in each move, we've been able to purchase homes without fear of being overextended, and we've been able to enjoy vacations when the Air Force says we get the time off. And when the kids head off to college, we feel prepared to tackle the ever-rising costs of higher education. In the end, my business has truly strengthened our family in a variety of ways.

SERVE

Do it for Your Community

Although it may seem like a decision about personal gain to start a business, I would argue that there are numerous benefits to the larger community that are worth considering. First, as we've just stated, the more *milpreneurs* there are in the world, the better chances for living a happier life with a stronger and more financially stable family unit. With happier individuals and stronger families, the less likely it is that an individual will retire early or separate from the military, and the more likely they are to continue to *serve*. This promotes higher retention rates at a time when our community is weary from the long-running US presence in the war in Afghanistan since 2001. With no end in sight to our military commitments, additional retention is even more important.

On top of that, I can only imagine the good works that will come from the service-minded objectives that *milpreneurs* pursue. Just within the ten years I have been active as a *milpreneur* I've been able to pay my success forward financially to support military spouse micro-loans, the endowment for the Air Force Academy, and military widows' retreats. That is a significant reinvestment in the military community that would amplify to a much larger extent with a significant rise in *milpreneurship*.

I am proud to say that if I were to die tomorrow, I would leave feeling fulfilled because of the opportunities my business (well, that and my awesome family!) has provided me. In fact, together with one of my best friends in life, Jamie Petersen, we've built a dream team of entrepreneurs and *milpreneurs*, called Team G.i.V.e. (Genuine.Inspired.Vibrant. Entrepreneurs). On the team, we jointly believe that we can be more, do more, and achieve more, when we keep our focus on giving back.

I am so proud of this team and how my business helps me *serve* my values and my WHY. Each year, our team of GiVers pushes themselves to achieve their very best sales performance for an important three-month period. Each GiVer pushes extra hard to earn additional money that they donate to an amazing summer camp for kids who have lost their fathers in military service. The camp is hosted by an organization called Knights of Heroes and over the years it has become very near and dear to our hearts.

The Knights of Heroes group was started by fellow Air Force Academy pilots as a way to honor the children of their fallen Air Force friend. The camp, which was founded in 2007 by Lt. Col. Steve Harrold, has grown tremendously since its inception and it is funded entirely by generous donations. Each summer, these kids have the opportunity to attend a weeklong respite session in the Rocky Mountains of Colorado where they hike, white water raft, mountain climb, and get valuable time with adult mentors (who also volunteer their time). Knowing several of the campers and their stories of hardship and regrowth, I am always inspired...inspired by the resilient spirit of children and the power of a loving family, inspired by those who serve something larger than themselves, and inspired to grow my business so that I can continue to *serve*.

Once we can tip the scales with enough *milpreneurs* to start a movement, more and more individuals will be inspired and gain the confidence that they can do it too, in their own communities. Think of the massive ripple effect a *milpreneur* movement could achieve!

GROW

Do it for Your Country

Milpreneurs who are inspired to start businesses today have the awesome chance to make a lasting impression on future generations. Obviously, my grandfather's business after his service in WWII inspired several generations of businesses after him. He had an influence on my parents who started their own business, and they in turn helped shape my businesses today. I wouldn't be surprised if my children follow suit as well. That is a wonderful ripple that began with just one key decision to "go for it" over fifty years ago.

With enough *milpreneur* start-ups like my grandfather's, we could strengthen the economy by providing more jobs and more income contributions. First, with more military spouse start-ups, we could begin to reverse the shocking 90% underemployment rate military spouses face now. With more spouses gainfully self-employed, we could begin chipping away at the estimated bill of up to one million dollars that military spouse underemployment is costing the country...and all this without needing government handouts or entitlements.

And that's just the beginning. When you consider the second-order effects of jobs created from new military start-ups, the possibilities for economic growth are literally endless.

Do it to Leave a Legacy

So, I want to ask you again. What will your legacy in this life be?

Will people say, "She spent a lifetime waiting for the right moment to shine and wishing the circumstances would change?"

Or will it be, "She ran after her dreams without looking back. She was committed to paying her success forward and she inspired a whole bunch of people along the way!"

After reading this book, you have everything you need to make your life's legacy meaningful and to be a part of the *milpreneur* movement. So, get started today.

Go and build something amazing. Follow your dreams. Connect with your military community and join the tribe of *milpreneurs* doing the same. Just get out there and make your mark on this world. Whether it's a ripple effect or a tidal wave, you *can* make a difference. Go change the world. You have the tools, skills, motivation, and now the support to do it.

So, get out there and discover that there is an entire world of opportunity to Live, Give, Serve and Grow...it's just waiting for *you*!

Conclusion

Thank you for taking a step forward in your journey and joining our *milpreneur* movement by reading this book. I hope that through these pages you have seen that any ordinary person with an idea, and the desire to LIVE, GIVE, SERVE and GROW can create small ripples in business that can amount to big change.

Whether you are military or not, you'll find many ways to apply what you've gained through these *milpreneur* stories:

Someone in your life may struggle to find flexible work that fits into his or her unusual situation.

Someone will find it difficult to find the WHY that drives them.

Someone struggles with the fears that hold them back.

Someone wonders how to juggle it all.

Someone needs resources to help them get a jump start.

And someone will be under-represented and need guidance on how to help themselves.

Whether that person is you or someone else, you now have the tools to inspire change in their personal situation.

But don't stop there.

What if you continued to think even bigger. Zoom out and take a 10,000-foot look at the larger influence you can have on your community with your newfound excitement. Think about it. With this new knowledge and a clear WHY, you have the power to start your *own* movement. Maybe you have people within your own sphere of influence you can support with your business idea. Maybe you already have resources you can share to educate people through a new blog. Or, maybe you can influence policy around a cause that you care about by providing a needed product, service, or education. Whatever this book inspired you to do, take the first step now. Don't wait for the perfect moment or circumstances to make your first move. Follow that WHY and start today.

I told you when we first met that I was on a mission...a mission to give back to our country's amazingly talented military community by showing them the value of starting and owning their own business. And now here we are. This book was a major step forward in progressing the *milpreneur* cause and we've gained *you* as a valued member of our growing tribe. The change we dreamed of is *happening*.

So, now it's your turn.

What mission is calling you? What change will *you* create?

Begin by exploring how you can build a business that can create change in your community. Teach yourself to stand up to the cultural norms, fears and indifference that hold us hostage to improving. Keep learning, growing and developing to get better and stay sharp. And never ever forget to turn around and give back to those behind you so the ripple of change can continue.

We hope you'll continue to remain a part of our *milpreneur* tribe and connect with us online as we help develop, encourage, and celebrate your future successes. We can't wait to help you say, "Mission Accomplished!"

Endnotes

Chapter 1

1. Claire Zillman, "For military spouses, job hunt is a battlefield," *Forbes*, May 9, 2014, http://fortune. com/2014/05/09/for-military-spouses-job-hunt-is-a-battlefield/.

2. Nelson Lim and David Schulker, "Measuring Underemployment Among Military Spouses," RAND Corporation, 2010. Available at: http://www.rand.org/content/ dam/rand/pubs/monographs/2010/RAND_MG918.pdf. (short title: "Measuring Underemployment")

3. Blue Star Families, *Social Cost Analysis of the Unemployment and Underemployment of Military Spouses.* Salt Lake City: Sorenson, 2016. Available at: https:// bluestarfam.org/wp-content/uploads/2016/05/Social-Cost-Analysis-of-the-Unemployment-and-Underemployment-of-Military-Spouses_Final_4-5-1.pdf. (short title: *Social Cost Analysis*)

4. Nelson Lim and David Schulker, "Measuring Underemployment."

5. Claire Zillman, "For military spouses, job hunt is a battlefield," *Forbes*, May 9, 2014, http://fortune. com/2014/05/09/for-military-spouses-job-hunt-is-a-battlefield/.

6. Nelson Lim and David Schulker, "Measuring Underemployment."

7. Blue Star Families, *Social Cost Analysis*.

8. Robert Bossert and Janet Kemp, "Suicide Data Report 2012," Department of Veterans Affairs Mental Health Services Suicide Prevention Program, 2012. Available at: https://www.va.gov/opa/docs/suicide-data-report-2012-final.pdf.

9. Blue Star Families, *Social Cost Analysis*.

10. Ibid

11. Erin Dooley, "90% of Military Wives Jobless or Underemployed 'Not Acceptable,'" March 1, 2014, http://abcnews.go.com/Politics/90-military-wives-jobless-underemployed-acceptable/story?id=22720559.

12. Mark Rockefeller, "Why The Military Is The Best Entrepreneurship Training Program In America," *Forbes*, August 3, 2016, https://www.forbes.com/sites/marklrockefeller/2016/08/03/why-the-military-is-the-best-entrepreneurship-training-program-in-america/#45b63fa43d60.

13. Kimberly Weiseul, "Half of World War II's Veterans Started Businesses. Less than 5 Percent of Today's Veterans Do," *Slate*, October 10, 2016, http://www.slate.com/blogs/

moneybox/2016/10/10/fewer_veterans_are_becoming_
entrepreneurs_a_lot_fewer.html.

14. Ibid.

Chapter 2

15. Mahlon Apgar IV and John Keane, "New Business with the New Military," Harvard Business Review, Sept, 2004, Accessed May 7, 2017, https://hbr.org/2004/09/new-business-with-the-new-military.

16. Karen Klein, "The Bottom Line on Startup Failures," Bloomberg, March 4, 2002. Accessed May 7, 2017, https://www.bloomberg.com/news/articles/2002-03-03/the-bottom-line-on-startup-failures.

17. Jay Goltz, "The 10 Reasons Small Businesses Fail," New York Times, January 5, 2011. Accessed on May, 2017, https://www.bloomberg.com/news/articles/2002-03-03/the-bottom-line-on-startup-failures.

Chapter 3

18. Beth Stebner, "Workplace morale heads down: 70% of Americans negative about their jobs, Gallup, June 24, 2013. Accessed April 14, 2017, http://www.nydailynews.com/news/national/70-u-s-workers-hate-job-poll-article-1.1381297.

Chapter 4

19. Kevin McSpadden, "You Now Have a Shorter Attention Span Than a Goldfish," May 14, 2015. Accessed April 14, 2017, http://time.com/3858309/attention-spans-goldfish/.

Chapter 5

20. Mark Rockefeller, "Why The Military Is The Best Entrepreneurship Training Program In American," *Forbes*, August 3, 2016, https://www.forbes.com/sites/marklrockefeller/2016/08/03/why-the-military-is-the-best-entrepreneurship-training-program-in-america/#45b63fa43d60.

Chapter 7

21. Harrow, Ben. "Survey Reveals Employee Productivity Averages 2 hours and 53 minutes a day," February 11, 2016. https://www.vouchercloud.com/blog/office-worker-productivity/.

22. Ibid.

Chapter 9

23. Greenleaf, Robert. "Servant Leadership: A Journey Into the Nature of Legitimate Power and Greatneess." New York: Paulist Press, 1973.

24. Ibid.

25. Pofelt, Elaine. "Survey: Entrepreneurs are the Happiest People on the Planet," *Forbes*, March 5, 2014. https:// www.forbes.com/sites/elainepofeldt/2014/03/05/survey-entrepreneurs-are-happier-than-employees/.

Author Bio

J en Griswold is a former active duty Air Force officer who didn't want to have to choose between the traditional choices of a full-time job or stay-at-home motherhood. She knew there was a flexible solution somewhere in between and she found it by taking control of her own future and starting her own businesses. After several successful business ventures, Jen is pursuing her passion to educate other members of the military community on how they can find fulfillment through entrepreneurship too. And the best part? She incorporates the idea that service and giving are just as important to entrepreneurship as they are to military life. Jen lives in Arlington, Virginia with her pilot husband, Kevin, and their two kiddos, Cole and Ally.

Acknowledgments

It's funny. Over the years, I've had a lot of big dreams for myself, but oddly not one of them included writing a book. I suppose it's because I've never really "loved" the limelight and a book seems to land you squarely in it. However, as I've grown older and as I've collected experiences and wisdom as a *milpreneur*, I realized I'd better jump at the chance to share my ideas when I was presented the opportunity. As a member of the military community, I am constantly reminded that we never know how long our precious lives will last and I couldn't stand the thought of having all my thoughts on growing *milpreneurs* locked up in my brain for any longer. It was time I shared them with the world.

There is absolutely no way this book would have come together if it wasn't for my priceless better half, Kevin. Babe, you have put up with 20 years of my "big ideas" and my beautiful mess of a head and heart. As annoying and inconvenient as my ventures were to your very organized and regimented military mind, you supported me every step of the way, believing in a vision that you couldn't always see. You believed in me on days when I wasn't sure I believed in myself and you never once complained at picking up the extra work around the house during the many hours I was plunking away at the computer. I'm not sure there are enough "I adore you's" and "I love you's" out there to truly tell you how much you mean to me. So, thank you for everything. You are my rock and I love you to pieces.

To Cole and Ally, you two are the whole reason I jumped out of the traditional rat race. So many wonderful things have developed from that one important decision. I used to be scared that our military life might screw you up. Now I know that our crazy life is actually what has made you into the strong and amazing human beings you are today. You inspire me daily to be the best I can be for you and I thank you for loving me for who I am. I may not be a great cook or the craftiest Mom, but I hope this book shows you that I'm sharing my gifts with you in a different way. You are both such wonderful young adults. I can't wait to see what dreams you'll chase and I hope this book inspires you too.

To Mom, Dad, Allison and Mike, you are the people who molded me into what I am. I owe you everything for that. Even though we always lived states apart, I can always feel your support from anywhere. Thanks for the cheering and encouragement. You mean the world to me! And to my sweet Grandpa George, I hope you know what an inspiration you've been to me all my life. I hope this book makes you proud. I think Grandma would have loved it!

Thank you to all the people who agreed to do interviews and share their stories throughout this book. I am overjoyed to get to tell your beautiful journeys. And thank you for paving the way for so many *milpreneurs* who will come behind you!

Thanks to my good friend and veteran resource expert, Crystal Rowley, for giving me a head start on Chapter 8 with all her knowledge and experience after many years in and out of the military. Crystal, thanks for contributing to the book and for your many years of amazing help and guidance in business.

And last but not least, thank you to my wonderful friend Sandy Thompson. She was the one who carefully and tirelessly read every version, made every edit and helped develop every idea no matter how late at night I sent her something. Sandy, thanks for pouring into this with me. We have so much good stuff ahead!!

Thank you for reading.

In writing *Mission Entrepreneur*, Jen Griswold did her very best to produce the most accurate, well-written and mistake-free book. Yet, as with all things human (and certainly with books), mistakes are inevitable. Despite Jen's and the publisher's best efforts at proofreading and editing, some number of errors will emerge as the book is read by more and more people.

We ask for your help in producing a more perfect book by sending us any errors you discover at errata@mango.bz. We will strive to correct these errors in future editions of this book. Thank you in advance for your help.

CPSIA information can be obtained
at www.ICGtesting.com
Printed in the USA
BVOW09s0847210917
495379BV00001B/1/P